The Unmasking:
Black in America

A Must Read If You Really Want To Understand What Black Men Face In America

Larry D. McCullum PharmD, MDiv.

About the Author

Dr. McCullum was born in Hollandale, Mississippi to Louise McCullum and John McCullum, Jr. Although being born in Hollandale, his family lived early on in Greenville, Mississippi and later moved to Leland, Mississippi where he graduated High School. Dr. McCullum received his primary, secondary and initial post-secondary education in the State of Mississippi. While in primary school he was a product of bussing, a desegregation effort in the South, and was a part of the first graduation class in the State to graduate integrated (from 1st through 12th grades).

Dr. McCullum received a Bachelor's Degree in Chemistry from the predominantly white university, (Delta State University in Cleveland Mississippi. While at Delta State University, he was actively engaged academically, athletically and civically. He was a member of the University Student Senate, a member of the Varsity Track Team and chapter President of Alpha Phi Alpha, Inc.

After graduation from Delta State University, Dr. McCullum felt a strong internal desire to pursue a degree at a historically black college and university (HBCU). He fulfilled that desire by enrolling in Howard University, Washington, DC. Dr. McCullum received graduate training in Biochemistry and received a professional degree in Pharmacy while at Howard. He credits Howard University for what he describes as becoming self-authenticated.

While at Howard University, he met his, what was soon to be wife, Chanelle Scott. They later married after graduating from pharmacy school together. They have two children together, Alexis and Larry, Jr.

Sometime after graduating Howard University, Dr. McCullum went on to obtain a Master of Divinity from Drew University, Madison, New Jersey and a Doctorate of Pharmacy from Shenandoah University, Winchester, Virginia.

He and his wife currently reside in Piscataway, NJ.

CONTENTS

Acknowledgments

»» ———————— ««

Having lived a life full of challenges, opportunities, and transitions that have served to shape, mold and mature me, I have learned to thank God for the benefits of life.

In particular, I am blessed and most grateful for my wife, Chanelle who has always supported me through thick and thin!

I thank the Lord for blessing me with three beautiful children: Cymora, Alexis, and Larry, Jr. They are the precious jewels of my life over which God alone has given me stewardship. I love them dearly, for they are the breath within my lungs and the smile upon my countenance. They are the motivation to be all that God has called me to be, for I understand that the blessings of the father will pass along to the children.

I thank God for the exploratory years of my life as well, for it was through these years that I came to know Him as my shield and my fortress.

I acknowledge foremost, my precious and dearest mother, Louise McCullum, who demonstrated the meaning of a living epistle. It was through her silent prayers and informing gazes that I continued to press forward through the oppressive forces of rural Mississippi, to live a life that she and my ancestors deserve.

I acknowledge and bless God always for my biological Father upon this earth, John McCullum, Jr. who, through his resilience and determination to be a provider for his entire family, taught me the importance of being there for my family as well.

Lastly, I thank God for a whole host of friends and acquaintances, who poked, prodded, pressed, and pulled me in every direction; for through it all, the contents of this book was made manifest. God bless you mightily

CHAPTER 1

The Invisible Mask We Wear

»» ———————————— «««

In this Covid-19 era, the entire world has been forced to shift from its daily norm. No longer are we have to move about freely; no longer are we able to do whatever come and go as we feel! Life has come almost to an abrupt halt! We've been forced to shelter in place or quarantine in order to slow the spread of this virus so that our healthcare systems will not be overwhelmed and to give time for our scientists to develop a vaccine or a cure! We are all, regardless of age, have be forced to rely on technology (Skype, Zoom, Face Book Live, etc.) to have group interaction. Our brick and mortar schools and universities are now educating their student's online! We have been forced to wear masks when in public and to keep a distance of six feet when we are in the presence of people!

Our minds and the attention of many, have been fixed on the events of this pandemic. The very airways are being

3

saturated with and traversed with constant updates about the Coronavirus! How many new cases there are! How many people have died from the Coronavirus: Have we flattened the curve? Is the curve declining? Is the curve increasing? This has become the new norm and now the entire world has become skilled at wearing masks because it is there lifeline; their defense against this invisible enemy! The mask, though uncomfortable, is a necessity. Though it might be burdensome and prevents us from breathing freely, it is allowing us to remain coronavirus-free! It is only through the wearing of the mask that we are able to survive during these times!

Much like the guidelines for survival during this pandemic, men of color have been forced to wear a mask, an invisible mask, for their entire lives. We are forced to wear these invisible masks to navigate the pitfalls, the threats to our well-being; the police; our jobs and even while we are shopping at establishments all as a means of survival! It is the invisible masks that allow men of color to exists within this society, even when there is no threat of a pandemic!

The invisible masks allows us to move about within corporate circles; within environments of influence, never really being able to show our true feelings or behave in a manner of which we are most comfortable for fear of how others will take it or for fear of whether our image may be threatening to others so we hide behind it! Though, the mask may be uncomfortable we must wear it! It is our defense against a visible enemy! The mask, though uncomfortable, is a necessity. Though it might be burdensome and prevents us from breathing freely, it is allowing us to support our families! The mask has been our life-line and It is only through the wearing of the mask that we have been able to survive throughout time in these United States of America! The United States of America, the land of the free; the home of the brave! Though people of color have long been brave, we have not really been free! Our reality is different than that of even the lowest white man who even he does not know that the system is using him to divide and conquer so that the very rich can remain on top. In the words of Lyndon B. Johnson: "If you can convince the lowest white man he's better than the best colored man, he won't know you're picking his pocket.

Hell, give him someone to look down on and he'll empty his pockets for you." It is this diabolical sentiment and others like it, that have resulted in the systematic oppression and disenfranchisement of people of color! It creates division and promotes hate all of which are contrary to what this country proclaims to stand for! It is this systematic oppression of people of color; the creation of the other; the unwanted; a people to be feared, oppression and held down that results in us needing to wear the mask as a very means of survival!

We are most often than not racially profiled! We are disproportionately targeted and criminalized by police. We have drugs planted on us by police. We are harassed while at shopping malls and always viewed as not being able to afford things while many of the other races are assumed to be wealthy, civil, and non-criminal. This is the white privilege that escapes us and that remains foreign to our people and is contradictory to what the United States of America pretends to be!

This contradiction of life and freedom that exists in the United States of America must stop! This fear of and degradation of people of color must stop! We are just as American as the next man! We have helped to make this country the richest in the world and without us there would not be a United States! No longer do we want to exist in America under these circumstances but until something changes, we will continue to wear the invisible mask!

What we endure: With the mask, it is hard to breath! It dampens our strength and causes us to move at a reduced pace in order to conserve energy to fight another day! With the mask it requires us to be mentally strong in order to quench the fiery darts of the enemy; to rise up every morning and face another day of societal warfare! It is only through the wearing of the mask that we are able to maintain a sanity to take life one day at a time! Day by day we endure the stereotypes; we endure the marginalization and minimalization! We see but do not overtly react to the lack of acknowledgement by our colleagues of a different hue. We steer clear of those that look like us for fear that if we are seen talking to more than one other black person it would look like we are conspiring and the end result would be retaliation. We are all too careful to speak in a soft and respectful voice with an intriguing tone as to not appear a threat to their privileged authority. We walk with a mild gait and timid stature in order to fit in and to be present but not overbearing for fear of invoking their perspective of being "not in our place". When there are team meetings that may rise to spirited discussions, we are careful not to be appear anger as to not validate the stereotypes of us being angry!

We always work with this hidden fear in the back of our minds that if the business does not do well, we will be as they say, "last hired first hired" or to be state it in a more colloquial way, "If you are black you stay back"! This is an unfortunate reality but it is very apropos in describing the landscape on which we move. We understand that we have to be, as our parents told us, five times as good to compete with even the average non-white. We understand the uphill battle we face and the systematic land mines we have to navigate just to walk through the doors of corporate America. We know very well that if we manage to walk through the doors that we must move cautiously and even "dumb it down" if you will so as to not intimidate the intelligence the others if we hope to stay there.

No, we don't all rap! Not all of us can dance! We all are not good at basketball or sports in general! We don't it chicken (though personally I love chicken—smile! We don't all have criminal records (in fact many of those that do, do so by no real fault of their own). We don't all come from troubled zip codes and even if we did, it does not define who we are! It's not how you start but how you finish! Some of us, in fact a more than you think, are just intelligent! We love being and using whatever God-given talent we have to contribute to society and to the shock of many, it could be fencing, swimming, inventing, physics, engineering, race car driving, skiing, bobsledding, etc. We are multi-talented and the color of our skin does not limit us.

In spite of it all, we manage to navigate the pitfalls of corporate America. In spite of all of this we, somehow, still manage to climb and climb and climb until we hit that glass ceiling and if we manage to shatter that glass ceiling, we are still not able to remove the mask. We press on; forging a way for the next person of color despite being weighed down, heavy, exhausted and overwhelmed not just because of the job but because of the extra energy required to wear the mask! The mask restricts oxygen and adds to the burden!

What we want: We want to be seen! We want to be heard! We want to be acknowledged! We want to be given a fair chance! Compete on an equal playing field! Yes, to all of this but dep down what we really want is to be a ourselves without fear of retaliation or threat of loss of life because others fear our blackness and/or our cultural differences!

For us, the security of our home is our safe haven; a place where we can take the mask off and finally be ourselves, however, due to wearing this invisible mask throughout the day and to virtually every place outside of your home, we find that there are other devastating effects! We find out that there is an accumulation of psychological and social pressures that impact not just us but now begin to affect our families! The accumulation of stress on us; the effects not being able to be ourselves; the weight of wearing the mask creates this dysfunctionality within what we thought was our safe place and as such now poses are threat to the next generation!

We are too tired to interact with our families for a period of time! We need dedicated time to decompress and take the weight off before we can interact lovingly with our families! It is hard to smile at your children because in the back of our minds we are retracing your steps at the job looking for any mistakes you may have made that would put you in a negative light or position at your job; we can't be all there for our children! Needing hours away from your family to regroup and unpack everything so that the needless worries of our day and the stress and pain that comes with it is not transferred into your household! Taking time to unwind so that we do not project on your loved ones the disrespect and disregard that we may have suffered while trying to provide for your family!

The mask is suffocating and the result is a social distancing that can invoke irreparable damage on your psyche and create a level of dysfunctionality on your family that can impact generations. My fear is that we are suffering from undiagnosed PTSD! We are in a war zone and our hope is that the damage we endure does not result is family casualty!

Lastly, if all of what you have read thus far reminds you of the Southern United States in the 1950's, you would not be wrong. It is very much akin to the Jim Crow era. The time is different but the rules are much the same. Having grown up in the deep South in the seventies, I know full well the experience and the ravaging effects of a racially divided nation. In 1954, segregation was deemed unconstitutional but it wasn't until I was in the second grade (1971) that my school was integrated. It was almost twenty years after the Supreme Court decision and Mississippi was still integrating its school systems! Here's something even shocking, in Mississippi today, the year 2020, some Mississippi schools are still being integrated! We wear an invisible mask to survive and succeed, while they wear the mask to disrupted, denigrate and destroy us as a people!

CHAPTER 2

Black in America

>» ——————————— «<

America is seen as "the way up"; "the promised land" for not only the poor in third world countries, but for the poor in most European countries as well. America, the land of opportunity is for many, the answer to economic disparity within their homelands, the way to move up the social scale, the way to pull themselves up by their "bootstraps".

In search of a hope for a brighter future, so many, particular those who lived near the American shores, risk their lives in make-shift boats, attempting to cross dangerous waters in an effort to reach this purported land of opportunity. However, what is the reality for those who reach its borders and integrate into its society? For the majority, the hope of realizing the American dream diminishes, and many are left with nowhere to turn. They are trapped between the land that was and the land promised. If they make within US borders, they began shortly thereafter to experience the reality of it all. Opportunity exists but the measure of its costs may still be one of devastation.

For those who had risked it all to find new found freedom in this land of opportunity, here are some questions for you: have you forgotten, have you not been taught, or are you unaware of the methods the overseers of this new found land used to elevate themselves to economic promise? Are you unaware, that the same country you seek to contribute your talents and service to (in hopes of financial reward); is the same country that has a history of enslaving and oppressing minorities, despite many of them being the castaways; the relegates of European lower class who now suffer memory loss and seek to relegate others to their previous state for fear of them returning to what was their reality? Are you unaware that the very country to which they sought refuge was the very cause of them having to do so? This country, through its various policies and treaties, works systematically to ensure that underprivileged nations are underdeveloped, pushing its people to look for solace in other lands of promise.

This new found land, America, is a construct arising from a patriarchal, imperialistic culture that has sought to dominate and exert its will on the entire world throughout history. From Alexander the Great to Napoleon, from Columbus to Cortez, the posture of the culture has been to search out and dominate all in the name of their God, and in search of wealth and riches at any cost. "Take it by force" has been their historical mantra.

The unfortunate truth faced by immigrants to this nation, specifically immigrants of color, is that the land of opportunity and freedom is really a robust system that maintains wealth for a few white men and their families. The unfortunate reality is that the top one percent in America owns over ninety percent of all wealth. This unequal distribution of wealth indicates a major social inequality for the vast majority of U.S. households. It is evident from these statistics that there exists a system within America that promotes the rich and denigrates the poor working class.

For minority Americans born within its borders, classism, racism, sexism, or any other form of systematic oppression is not a surprise. For so many grueling years, generations have been subjected to hard labor amidst racist and discriminative laws, post chattel slavery laws that resulted in families merely etching out a living, while the elite wealthy white Americans work within a system that was designed to create and maintain generational wealth.

History tells of chattel slavery, transferrable human property, i.e. transferable wealth from generation to generation for white slave owners. History speaks of colonialism and its devastating effects upon the native people of this country. History also speaks of Jim Crow Laws, Union discrimination and racism, systematically designed to oppress the poor while shielding the white dominant class. America, throughout history, is undoubtedly a land of opportunity for all, but at its core a heartless, selfish, insensitive imperialistic system of oppression and greed, that has no regard for the common good.

As years passed, new technologies were developed, and new means of ensuring the socio-economic position of the wealthy were sought out. As though political, legal and corporate disparities in this country alone were not enough, this system of economic disparity seeks to exercise its control on global markets as well. In an article entitled *"The ABCs of The Global Economy"* by The Dollars and Sense Collective, March/April 2000, chapter 3; U.S. corporations are on a corporate offensive. "Corporate America pursue profits in a worldwide global economy. Instead of producing goods in the U.S. to export, they move more and more toward producing goods overseas…" This strategy not only has a major impact on the U.S. economy, in that the poor struggling underclass of America will struggle even more through loss of job opportunities, but it also impacts the economies of the countries in which these countries seek to operate. More often than not, these corporations seek to protect their interest by compelling governments to "tax, regulate and subsidize foreign businesses exactly as they would their local businesses," for any losses in profit due to changes in public policy. U.S. corporations in international markets controlling international governments, resemble colonialism and imperialism, irrespective of the fact that it is being done under the guise of capitalism.

It has been made clear that a highly organized system exists within America, designed to benefit the wealthy, while oppressing the less fortunate. But, how can it be stopped or at the very least circumvented so that the American dream can be more than just a pipe dream? How can this country move to a system where equity for all regardless of race, creed or color?

The upper class in America controls the nation's wealth and, by direct correlation, they also control the nation's power. They either hold positions of power or indirectly have influence over these positions. As long as this unequal distribution of power remains in place, the hopes of creating a fair and equal opportunity system for all American's remain bleak.

Being a minority in America, one is relegated, largely, to the lower class. Systematic racism, institutionalization and disenfranchisement are the invisible walls that enclose them. For many, it is like living life in a pressure cooker, you're enclosed in these walls of systematic disenfranchisement. The pressure of being enclosed seeks to break your will and melts away the hope one has! When you been in the cooker for so long, your dreams; your desires; your vision; your plans all seem to evaporate away! This is a systematic discriminatory pressure cooker and for centuries its purpose has been the same—to kill you off or at the very least isolate you from society! The pressure cooker is not safe! It is dangerous and only by controlling the temperature and releasing its straps can be pressure and its devastating effects be relieved!

I believe the hope of a better future for minorities lie in education. More minorities are graduating from college now than in times past. With increases in minority education, along with a steady rise in the minority population, it is projected that there will be a reversal in the nation's demographics in the near future. It has been projected that by the middle of the twenty-first century, the minorities of today will be the majority of tomorrow. Not only will the sheer numbers increase demographically, but also the number of these individuals educated will increase as well, resulting in a much more empowered group into the marketplace. Undoubtedly, these individuals will be poised to contribute to the economy and to society. But, will this be enough to shift the existing power structure? It is not income alone that will close socio-economic gaps; income must be accompanied by the building of wealth. Wealth is transferrable and will serve to maintain higher social positions for those who inherit it. Therefore, along with the demographic paradigm shift that is to occur, a corresponding strategy for increasing wealth must be employed in order for any true gains to be realized.

Additionally, there will be a need for organized groups to lead this transformation that will obviously take place. The groups must be unselfish and have a spirit of sacrifice. They must work for the common and greater good of the people. Historically, within the minority communities, the church has assumed this role. But, should it be the role of the church to help correct socio-economic injustices that are prevalent in America? On the other hand, one could ask, "Is it solely the role of political groups to advocate change within a political system?" I strongly believe that in order to tackle such a monster, a strategic allegiance between these two groups and other support groups, is required. Religious groups through education, emancipation, and empowerment measures can assist families in their efforts to raise their IQ, as well as to exhort an otherwise disparate group possessing minimal hope, to step out and reach for more. Political groups can continue to fight for laws and social programs that benefit the lower classes within America, as well as providing opportunities for equalized wealth throughout class groups. However, even with a coalition of religious and political organizations, and an impending paradigm shift in the nation's demographics, the tasks at hand is great. However, to sit by idly and do nothing while the wealthy gets wealthier is not an option. The minority groups of tomorrow must continue to prepare themselves academically, as well as to align themselves in a way that is insistent on liberation, economic freedom and opportunity for all.

I have taken the time to explain the bright attractions of America to you as well as lay a foundation of the forces at work within America that contradicts those bright attractions. I have not only attempted to shed light on the crisis that exists within these United States of America for minorities at large, but to lay the foundation to further explore the travesty of crisis for a certain group in particular—the African American male and his community. Please read further as I begin to chip away at the forces that hinder the African American male from truly integrating into American society, as well as explore ways to restore the African male to his prominent place with family, community, and within the nation. And to help us remove the mask we wear!

CHAPTER 3

Generational Pain

»» ———————— ««

An underlying cause of the pain we feel deep down is generational. It is a deep cutting, deeply scaring pain that has its roots in slavery and that continued through chattel slavery—a systematic government-sanctioned brutal and dehumanizing way of oppression from generation to generation. This system is the face of the emotional and psychological pain that the descendants of the system carry. It was as legal system and that in itself makes it all the worse. Legalization legitimizes the system and it so doing it sends the message that we (the government) do not hold you to be of value. It relegates us to the position of less than and is a scourge of our esteem and self-worth, hence we hide! We hide behind a mask that we hope to free us of this pain! We hide behind a mask so that we won't have to confront the pain that still wreaks havoc within us and has done so to our families over generations. Here are the particulars of the system.

The Chattel System was a legal institution of human chattel enslavement, primarily of Africans and African Americans, that existed in the United States of America in the 18th and 19th centuries after it gained independence and before the end of the American Civil War.

Slavery had been practiced in British North America from early colonial days, and was legal in all thirteen colonies at the time of the Declaration of Independence in 1776. By the time of the American Revolution (1775–1783), the status of slaves had been institutionalized as a racial caste associated with African ancestry. When the United States Constitution was ratified (1789), a relatively small number of free people of color were among the voting citizens (mainly property owners).

Between 1650 and 1860, approximately 10 to 15 million enslaved people were transported from western Africa to the Americas. Most were shipped to the West Indies, Central

America, and South America. From Senegal, Sierra Leon, Congo, Angola (Senegambia Region)

Europe: .3 million, North America: 0.5 million, West Indies: 4.5 million, Central America (Guatemala,), South America (estimated to be between 10 to 12 million by some sources). You see, most were shipped to Brazil (some estimates say about 10 million making Brazil the second largest population of blacks in the world; second only to the continent of Africa). Only about 500 thousand were actually shipped to North America but the number of African descendants grew with the onset of cotton, tobacco, rice farming, etc. in what was to become the United States.

In the North American cities of Boston, New York, Philadelphia whale oil, lumber, furs were produced and supplied to England. Charleston, SC produced rice, silk, indigo, tobacco and traded it to England and then from England rum, iron, gunpowder, cloth and tools were sent to Africa to keep dividing our people and fueling tribal conflict that would in turn provide more slaves for capture and export. From Africa: Slaves to West Indies and Europe; gold, ivory, spices, and hardwoods to England. From the West Indies: slaves to Charleston, SC and Boston, New York, Philadelphia then sugar and molasses to Boston, New York, and Philadelphia ports. All of this made up the triangular trade routes (from Africa to North America, the West Indies and Europe) and it was the vast majority of the world economy. It was profitable, though shameful, demeaning and wrong!

It is important for us to know that our ancestors were not born Slaves! They were not born to be tools or instruments for profit! They were born free and subsequently those of European descent, with the help of carefully manipulated African tribes, captured and made slaves! Slaves were created not born!

If you tap into your sense of humanity and reflect on this, you can't help but ask the question: What would make a human being believe that he/she can take the freedom of another human being and deprive them of their God-given rights? Well, here are the basis for this type of thinking and it was couched in a perverted Christian hermeneutical interpretation and selfish adaptation of the bible. There was a newly versioned concept of Christianity, a code from them to live by. It starts off seemingly reasonable but then progressively becomes perverse:

- Christians participated in everyday life and shared social and cultural world with non-Christian neighbors.

- They also had common questions concerning the place of women, the roles of slaveholders and slaves, the legitimacy of itinerant preachers, and sexuality.

- Christianity in the West (America) received from Roman culture ideas of the ideal body that informed their notion of the "the Christian body"

  o The ideal body was controlled through diet and the limitation of sexual activity, a body whose practices and habits were carefully chosen.

  o The ideal body was everything that slave bodies were not and could not be, for slaves were reduced to bodies

- By law, sexual coercion on a slave could not be considered rape

- Slaves could be tortured in ways that citizens could not.

- Slave collars were adorned with crosses

It's hard to believe but this perverted way of looking at people that do not look like them through this version of Christianity makes it easy for them to elevate themselves and denigrate others. They feel that it is their god given right to always be on top no matter what it takes! It makes them feel like they are superior to all others and everyone should bow down to them. In their mind it is their birthright and god gave it to them. Unfortunately, this perverted attitude, this pervert belief system is shared from generation to generation and is often triangulated in their societal systems in order to give it strength to continue to wreak havoc on any who do not look like them. And unfortunately, this carries still today:

CHAPTER 4

Slavery by Another Name

In the previous chapter, I discussed how the slave trade was predicated upon a triangulated infrastructure which allowed for sustainability and strength. I closed that chapter asserting that a similar triangulated infrastructure still exists today. It is this triangulated, camouflaged in a political system controlled by the wealthy that still has embedded within it the need for subjugation in order to bring out the benefits of wealth for the aristocrats of today. Goods are still required to exchange for free labor which in turn generates profits for the top one percent of the population. The free labor is this infrastructure is no longer called slaves by name but instead are incarcerated, denigrated, violated and incriminated in a system that once they are released found themselves trapped in a triangulated system that operates like an endless revolving door in their lives, oftentimes denying the basic human rights; loss of voting rights and devoid of civil liberties. It is de facto slavery—slavery by another name.

Critical to the survive of this system is the need for a lower class. One that will tow the line of menial work! One that can be characterized as the valueless, meaningless and animalistic. This characterization is critical to the success and survival of the system because it keeps the ninety-nine percent divided; fighting against each other so that the exploitation of the masses by the few can go unnoticed.

In order to see the effects of this system, you needn't look too far to see video segments of black men and women acting out in what the media deems animalistic behavior but what in reality they are crying out for help and to be noticed and recognized as being human. They are acting out destructively because they feel as though they don't have everywhere to turn and that no one understands them nor their plight. They are being destructive because the pain that systematic oppression and marginalization has dealt is swelling up so greatly inside that they feel a great need to release it. So, they project that hurt, that pain on society; they project it on others if only to feel a sense of relief if only for a little while. They feel like cutting some things off inside them but they instead cut off the lives of anyone that's near!

As unfortunate as it is, as sad as it may be, it becomes therapeutic this behavior providing a way to face the day.

Deep down the world they live in is disruptive so they project their disruptive world upon the world at large! They effect is a mischaracterization of behavior as animalistic but in actuality what it is a psychologically and emotional characterization that requires professional treatment but the media and those who are the source of the pain choose to call it animalistic behavior because it helps to sustain the power structure needed to benefit the powerful few.

What many are experiencing can be liken unto a child who has sought the affection, attention and love of a parent endlessly but never to receive it! He/she eventually grows up devoid of emotion, lacking empathy and as a result there is repressed anger that overflows onto the rest of society causing damage.

If we really were to conduct a psychological assessment, I'm sure what we might find is a diagnosis of PTSD. It is Post Traumatic Stress that is the rooted cause of this dysfunctionality. A diagnosed of PTSD requires professional help. It does not require imprisonment and criminalization. However, those in positions of power view the actions of the afflicted not with empathy but with a diabolical disdain for black men. Misnaming and mischaracterizing the behavior as animalistic serves a purpose! Why? Because it suits them! It benefits them! It is profitable to them! Hence, we say weekly if not daily modern-day lynching of black men because if benefits the system.

We are still being lynched today! if we do not conform to the expectations of those who refuse to acknowledge our humanity and to respect our human rights and civil liberties and that we are born free; the result is a modern-day lynching! It only takes an African-American male deciding to jog in a public neighborhood that could and in fact has resulted in their murder by white vigilantes who belief they are exercising their government sanctioned white privilege to deprive a black person of the civil liberties! It only takes one black person to lose track of his "place" in America by obtaining a license to carry a firearm and then being pulled over by police, identifying that he has a license to carrying, attempting to retrieve the license to present to the office and the result is the loss of his life. It only takes a black male to sit peacefully in his car, only to be harassed by a police officer, detained illegally and treated like a dog because he asked why he is being detained! It only takes a black male flagging down a police officer to ask for help because his car broke down to be gun down like an animal! It only takes a 12-year-old black boy playing with a play gun to be gunned down by police within three seconds while white vigilantes and white gun rights activists can protest carrying AR-7 with stock and other heavy weapons despite police presence! It only takes black men and women worshipping in a church to extend God's Grace and loving-kindness to a white male only to be murdered by that white male and the police demonstrating constraint and care to the white male as opposed to the families of those slain! I can go on and on and on with examples of the blatant disregard for black human life in

American and the subsequent dehumanization of an entire race! It only takes a black male selling loosies (single cigarettes) on the streets of Staten Island, NY to be bound in a choke whole and despite crying out "I can't breathe" is continually strangled until loss of life! It only takes one black male on the streets of Minneapolis Minnesota to be told to get out of his car and after complying having one of four police officers who have been sworn to protect and serve apply his knee to the neck of the a compliant black male for over nine minutes with so much force it results in loss of life! There is an obvious hate for black men in this country! The result is a denial of humanity; a criminalization of and a dehumanization of black men! It is this general characterization, slavery by another name, that fuels the need for black men to wear an invisible mask in an attempt to dispel this characterization; to survive in this war-zone of America and to experience some aspect of human decency!

CHAPTER 5

WE are Family!

»» ———————— ««

Contrary to what the media depicts! Contrary to how we are portrayed, innate to every African American male is the need to be part of a family. It is this spirit of the African ideals regarding family and community that resides in each and every last one of us. We are human with human needs! We need to be free of the invisible mask in order to live freely with our families and our community!

The tradition of African people is one that embraces close-knit communities where everyone, the African male in particular, is expected to live a life that sacrifices for the greater good of the community. A close family unit is essential, and it exists so that all might contribute to the betterment of the greater community. We are human!

This African ideal regarding family and community has been transferred to or inherited by their descendants. It is encoded within our DNA the ideals of family and the importance of community. The African American male by nature has an attitude of reverence towards family and community. For the African American male, the family and community are the places where his identity is established and affirmed. It is within the family and community where his net worth is gained and shared. We are human!

Traditionally, the role of man within the family has placed him as a central figure. Therefore, it is expected and understood that his role within the family and community has to be one in which he actively contributes in a positive way. It should be understood that the male was to live a life of sacrifice for the greater good of the community. We are human!

For the African American male, there is an innate desire to belong to something greater! Some that traverses generations and lands and that elevates the next. This desire begins with, is supported by, and has been influenced by

African tradition, and by the African cultural belief system regarding family. We are human!

God almighty has created humankind to exist in relationship. The need to belong to a group or social structure is written upon the hearts of man by the creative finger of God. This notion of existing within community is evidenced throughout the sacred word of God and has been studied by many sociologist, systematic theologians and psychologists.

The mother must bond with her newborn child, or else there exists a chance that the child may be emotionally and/or mentally underdeveloped. (Bowlby 1958) In addition to mother-child bonding, the father plays an active role in the development of the child, which is equally important. The absence of the father within the family structure has been shown to have devastating consequences on the child's development, and may result in destructive behavior during adolescence and/or adulthood. (National Center for Children in Poverty) It is therefore within the human experience, the necessity of existing within family structure, for it lends to emotionally and mentally stable progeny. Ingrained in the male's DNA, particularly the African American male's DNA, is the need to belong and exist in relationship, which is critical to the emotional, intellectual and psychological health of his offspring, and ultimate the family and community. We are human!

The African American male has both a historical and present need to belong and operate within a tightly knit social system. His very existence within the community was sacrificial, and as such, he needed to contribute to the community and not be overly concerned with individual accomplishments, unless those accomplishments would have a positive impact on the community as a whole. Nancy Body Franklin in her book "Black Families in Therapy—Understanding the African American Experience" (2003), states, regarding the African American male, "to be human was to belong to the whole community". She goes on to say that the African male was largely concerned with doing "not something for the betterment of the individual, but rather something for the community of which the individual was an integral part". It is indeed ingrained in the DNA of African

American men not only to exist within community but also to contribute richly to it.

If we were to consider hard this family belief system, we would conclude that existence apart from community, or to be excluded from community and not being allowed the opportunity to actively contribute to community, can have grave and devastating consequences. If we were to reflect deeply, we will begin to understand that exclusion, marginalization, institutionalization and dehumanization has contributed to the breakdown of the African American male's positive role in society and has led to a dysfunctional family unit! He has been impacted emotionally, mentality and socially and it has had a devastating effect that could take generations to fully heal and to fully recover.

Looking closer at the impact we see that African American men are disproportionally incarcerated, unemployed and underemployed, and above all, disproportionally compensated for equal services conducted in equal positions as their Caucasian counterparts. Packed in jail cells like animals! Given prison sentences sometimes two times longer than a white man who committed the same crime. They are and have been systematically expelled from or prohibited from participating in American society. They have been victims of systematic efforts to remove us or expel us from the very country of their ancestors built through blood, sweat, tears and ingenuity.

One need only to take their blinders off and look closely to see the historical cause leading up to the present devastation of the African American family and community. The effects of systematic racism and the depiction of the black man as inhuman, destructive and animalistic is a direct and devastating against us! Looking carefully one can see better understand the cause of the family breakdown rampant in our communities.

This effects of institutionalization and marginalization is evidenced by a sense of aggravation; anxiety and anger that often is exhibited by African American men and the impact of these potentially dangerous emotions have wreaked havoc on the African American male and his family and community. It has resulted in an increase in crime, an increase in African

American suicides and a fundamental breakdown in the belief system that is ingrained within him. Thus, the biblical proverb: *"The fathers eat sour grapes, and the children's teeth are set on edge"* (KJV) is likely to have become flesh once again in the lives of God's people.

According to the U.S. Census Bureau, National Center for Health Statistics, Americans for Divorce Reform (www.divorcemag.com/statistics/statsUS.html), fatherless homes account for 63% of youth suicides, 90% of homeless/runaway children, 85% of children with behavior problems, 71% of high school dropouts, 85% of youths in prison, well over 50% of teen mothers. Additionally, 24% of the American population has never been married, indicating a major shift in the nation's attitude toward marriage and family.

In addition, there are startling statistics that point to African Americans. African Americans (28.5%) are about six times more likely than their Caucasian counterparts (4.4%) to be admitted to prison during their lifetime (U.S. Department of Justice). Based on current rates of incarceration, an estimated 7.9% of African American males compared to 0.7% of Caucasian males, will enter State or Federal prison by the time they are age 20, and 21.4% of African American males versus 1.4% of Caucasian males, will be incarcerated by age 30 (U.S. Department of Justice). The National Institute of Drug Abuse estimated that while 12 percent of drug users are African Americans, they make up nearly 50 percent of all drug possession arrests in the U.S.

This is the reality of how we are treated and depicted within these borders! This is a startlingly descriptive of how we are depicted, stereotyped and dehumanized so as to exclude us from full participation in the very country our ancestors gave their very lives to build! And this has become the very foundation by which the wearing of the invisible mask has become an unfortunate necessity. We are family and we need to exist in family else we are destined to survive by any means necessary!

From the African American perspective, we can see the need to wage war against the attacks on our communities and to uphold the importance of family and community! Sadly, but though certain, we may deduce that if the African American male is not afforded the opportunity to make a positive contribution to his family and community, as a means of survival, he is destined to wear a mask either in a positive way to live amongst the warfare or in a negative way that leads to death and destruction. Let's hope it's the former!

CHAPTER 6

Your History Does Not Begin with Slavery

»» ———————— ««

I embark upon this history lesson because it is needed! When any group or any people have their history stripped. When a group of people have the knowledge of their ancestry stripped and are forced to live with an identity that is a fabrication, the result is a loss of identity; a loss whom you really are and more drastically; it results in a lost nation! A people without their true identity are displaced and are foreigners in a strange land forced to live with the knowledge of who they are concealed. A concealing mask is forced upon them and it is through this mask they live with the very hope of the past fading.

Our history does not begin with slavery. Though we may be foreigners in a strange land, once we learn of our rich history and our contribution to building nations, we will begin to recapture not only our identity but our dignity, respect, value and self-authentication.

The modern-day perspective regarding the continent of Africa, regarding civilization, culture, economy and the like, Northeast Africa and South Africa notwithstanding, is that Africa is dark continent. A continent of poor, uncivilized, war-torn, heathen nations replete with AIDS, malaria, starvation, and a lack of technology. A continent that is in desperate need of rescue.

Images of Africa that are televised show largely the Serengeti, bush people, babies with swollen bellies, or white missionaries teaching poorly dressed African children how to read and write. They depict markets that have make-shift food stands with fish covered in flies, strange cultural dishes that are being cooked on primitive looking cooking ware and various other unappetizing items. These are the images you see! You see videos of tribal wars, coup d'état's, Islamic wars and the like.

Never do you hear of the rich natural resources that once vastly covered the continent. You never hear of the spices indigenous to the area; the diamonds and other minerals native to the area or even the wonders of its ancient civilizations forged by ancient kingdoms such as the Kingdom of Ghana, Kingdom of Mali, Kingdom of Songhai, the Meroe Kingdom. The airways are not filled with this knowledge! If it is it is usually it is about Northeast Africa, a land captured and claimed by Europeans to be their own because how can these people who they depict as uncivilized be responsible for created all of the glory of the area. Therefore, the splendor of Egypt; the pyramids at Giza; the golden sarcophagus of the pharaohs; the majesty of the pyramids and the precision in which they were built are relegated to the skill and knowledge of Europeans.

Often tied to the depiction of Egyptian wonders of the world is a question of how could the ancient cultures of Africa could have the architectural and mathematical minds to build such highly innovative and technological structures? These structures must have been created by aliens or perhaps a supreme being of foreign descent and of course these supposed supreme beings were white. Never could they have been built by the people indigenous to the area!

You see, if you control the image! If you control what people see! If you define what is good; what is intelligent; what success looks like! Conversely if you define what is bad! What is non-human; what is criminal; who will be the low class! If you as the ruling power control these things, then you have the power to control lives! You have the power to exclude or include; denigrate or elevate! You control the minds; the thinking of the masses, you have the power to determine how groups live! Of course, those in control have chosen those of a darker hue than they to live in the less. The problem is what they depict is not our historical reality.

For our knowledge, there was a plethora of ancient black civilizations throughout the world (The Minoans of Ancient Greece, the Indus Cush Civilization, the Olmec Civilization of Mexico, the Shang Dynasty of Ancient China, Ancient Mesopotamia, etc.), however, in order to maintain the brevity of this book, I will focus only on a few ancient black empires on the continent of Africa.

Who we were (The Golden Age)

The Golden Age of West Africa spans from the start of the eighth century to the end of the eighteenth century and highlights the overlapping great trading empires of: Ghana (700-1200), Mali (1200-1500), and Songhai (1350-1600). The best known of the Iron Age states is Ghana (no direct connection or geographic overlap with the modern nation of Ghana that gained its independence from Britain in 1957). Trans-Saharan Gold traders from the Ghana area formed the link between the important resources of salt from the northern part of Africa, and the gold from the sub-Saharan region. This connection integrated them into the Mediterranean world and its trade connections with the other classical civilizations. Their control of the trans-Saharan gold trade allowed them to fund a large army and rise to empire status.

The Empire of Mali: The empire of Mali stretched for thousands of miles from the west Atlantic coast of Africa across the sub-Saharan savanna. The empire was more developed and oversaw much more extensive agriculture than Ghana did. It was ruled by kings called Mansa. Ibn Battuta, a famous Muslim traveler, visited Mali 's capital in 1352, and described the rule of these Mansas this way:

The Negroes possess some admirable qualities. They are seldom unjust and have a greater abhorrence of injustice than other people. Their Mansa shows no mercy to anyone least guilty of the act of injustice. There is complete security in their country. Neither traveler nor inhabitant has anything to fear from robbers or men of violence.

The most famous Mansa of the empire of Mali was **Mansa Musa**. In 1324-1325, he made his hajj (pilgrimage to Mecca) which became very famous for the display of extravagance. It is recorded that he took 100 camels just to carry gold which he gave as gifts along the way. He was served by 500 servants. It is said that in Cairo (Egypt) he gave away so much gold that the surplus caused a destabilization of Egypt's economy. This famous pilgrimage was significant for it put Mali "on the map" of the medieval world as news of his wealth and extravagance spread quickly and brought attention to Mali. It placed Mali, in the eyes of the known world, as a great Empire rivaling that of Ghana. The Mali kings eventually lost power in the late 14th and early 15th century.

The ruling kingdom moved eastward to the kingdom of Songhai along the Niger River. The founder of this new empire was Sonni Ali, a self-proclaimed Muslim, although many questions his devotion to Islam and it appears that he exploited the religion to centralize his own political power (think of the combined roles of military, religious, and political authority taught by Islam). Ali was a military conqueror who was successful in using war boats along the Niger River and thus providing him control of the region.

The primary opposition to Sunni Ali's rule were the Muslim scholars at Timbuktu. Ali ruthlessly persecuted them when they challenged his power. The Songhai 's empire was came to an end in 1591 by invaders from Morocco. The Moroccan armies brought with them a new weapon that the Africans could not match- firearms! A first on the continent in Africa!

Timbuktu became an important trading and scholarly center in sub-Saharan Africa during the Mali and Songhai empires. It is located on the northern bend of the Niger River, the southern edge of the Sahara Desert. Here is a first-hand recorded account of Timbuktu by a Leo Africanus when he visited the city in the early 1500s.

There are many shops of craftsmen and merchants, especially of those who weave cotton and cloth. To this place merchants bring cloth from Europe. All the women of this area, except maidservants, go with their faces covered and sell all necessary kinds of food. The inhabitants of this area are very rich, so much so that the king has married both of his daughters to two rich merchants. The rich king has many articles of gold and keeps a magnificent and well-furnished court. When he travels anywhere, he rides a camel that is led by some of his noblemen. He travels likewise when he goes into war, and his warriors ride upon horses. Attending him he always has 3000 horsemen and a great number of foot soldiers armed with poisonous arrows. Here there are many doctors, judges, priests and other educated men that are well maintained at the kings' cost. Many manuscripts and books can be bought here and are sold here for more money than any other merchandise.

In its heyday, Timbuktu was an important trading hub for two of Africa's most important items of commerce: salt and gold. The wealth of the city is evident from the quotation above. But Timbuktu also became an important city for Islamic scholarship. Its Mosque contained a library and a university where scholars, theologians, and Muslim jurists studied. Thus, the most important trade in Timbuktu was in books.

The Kingdom of Kush, 1070 BC to 350 A.D, was an ancient kingdom in Nubia, located on the confluences of the Blue Nile, White Nile and River Atbara in what is now Sudan and South Sudan. The Kushite emperors ruled as pharaohs of the Twenty-fifth dynasty of Egypt for a century, until they were expelled by the Assyrians under the rule of Esarhaddon.

During classical antiquity, the Kushite imperial capital was at Meroe. In early Greek geography, the Meroitic kingdom was known as Ethiopia. The Kushite kingdom with its capital at Meroe persisted until the 4th century A.D, when it fell largely due to internal rebellion and was eventually captured and burnt to the ground by the Kingdom of Aksum.

The name *Kush,* since at least the time of Josephus (a first century A.D, Jewish Historian), has been connected with the biblical character Cush, in the Hebrew Bible, son of Ham (Genesis 10:6). Ham had four sons named: Cush, Put, Canaan and Mizraim (Hebrew name for Egypt). According to the Bible, Nimrod, a son of Cush, was the founder and king of Babylon, Erech, Akkad and Calneh, in Shinar (Gen 10:10). Kushites also built burial mounds and pyramids (even though today they are beneath the water trapped by the Aswan Dam in Aswan Egypt said to have been built to allow proper irrigation of lands and for hydroelectricity in the area).

As you can glean from the accounts of these Great Empires, there were periods of dominance, intellectualism, culture and economic prowess that existed on the continent of Africa. This history is devoid of and separate from any contribution from Europeans! In fact, it is because of the splendor of Africa which was noised throughout the known world, that Europeans began to set their sights eyes of envy on this great continent.

For Africans, all of the materialistic success meant nothing and would not be possible, if not for a deep belief in a higher power; a deep belief in God! Religion was of most important to them! Ancestral, Christianity, Jewish faith and Islam were a few of the religions practiced on the continent.

Most African tribes had similarities in their belief systems. They were animistic, believing in a world controlled by spiritual forces and gods. These forces had to be dealt with through a specialist who would proscribe rituals, sacrifices, or some other form of religious practice to affect events. These beliefs created a view of how the universe worked and how one should ethically relate oneself to it. In their belief system, their ancestors, the first settlers of the land, were the true owners of the land, and they had a continued spiritual role in harvests and fertility even after death. Thus, land was more than just a source of agriculture; it took on religious significance. So, to be separated from it, meant you were cut off from the very thing that tied you to your past; to be cut off from it would mean that you were even separated spiritually from your people.

Apart from animism, and apart from Islam that spread across north Africa, there remained "islands" of Christianity in the midst of its civilizations. Christianity came to Africa before Islam.

In fact, monotheistic thought (or the belief in one God) was formed and developed centuries before organized European religion escaped pluralism.

Consider as a backdrop to this, Genesis 12:1 God speaking to Abram and saying get up out of Haran and go to a land that I will show you and Abram left Haran and traveled into the land of Canaan. The land of Canaan the grandson of Noah and the brother of Cush, whose land was later known as the land of the Kushites which was to be later in the 4ᵗʰ century AD became known as the land of the Nubians, who are today inhabitants of the land of southern Egypt and central Sudan in Africa. The name *Kush*, since at least the time of Josephus (a first century Jewish Historian), has been connected with the biblical character Cush, in the Hebrew Bible (Hebrew: כוש), son of Ham (Genesis 10:6). Ham had four sons named: Cush, Put, Canaan and Mizraim (Hebrew name for Egypt). According to the Bible, Nimrod, a son of Cush, was the founder and king of Babylon, Erech, Akkad and Calneh, in Shinar (Gen 10:10).

Or perhaps consider the Pharaoh Akhenaten of the 18th dynasty of Egypt or perhaps even the Dagon people of Mali or the Ethiopians (These are all African countries, I might add) they all introduced the belief in monotheism to the world, the belief in one God.

Even today we know about the Limbe tribe of central Zimbabwe and South Africa, whose oral tradition states that their ancestors left what we now know as Israel some 2,500 years ago. They were Jews in the land of Canaan. The very same land where God told Abraham to journey.

If we move from monotheistic thought to the development of Christianity itself, we learn that the first Christians were Jews! Consider Acts 8:26, a passage about an Ethiopian Eunuch, a court official of Candace, queen of the Ethiopians who had come to Jerusalem to worship the Jewish and was returning home from celebrating the Passover, when the now Apostle Phillip came across him reading the book of Isaiah and ministered Jesus to him! It is said that it is this same

Ethiopian Eunuch, a Jew, who started the Coptic Church in Africa.

In support of this, we must consider Saint Mark's Coptic Orthodox Cathedral, Alexandria Egypt which was said to be founded by St. Mark himself not even 60 years after Jesus' resurrection and ascension (60 AD), you see evidence that Christianity as we know it was well established in Africa well before it had reached the European continent around the 4th century AD. It wasn't until over 300 years after the death and resurrection of Christ that you will find the development of Christianity into an organized faith, whose precepts would be espoused throughout the world.

European Christianity, if you will, found its roots in Northeast Africa with the likes of European Church Fathers who studied in Africa before taking this knowledge into Europe. European church fathers like Origen of Alexandria (who lived over 200 years after the death and resurrection of Christ, Athanasius of Alexandria (who lived 300 years after the death and resurrection of Christ), Justinian (who lived 500 years after the death and resurrection of Christ 527). Christianity was not birthed in Europe but was fundamentally birthed in the mother land of Africa. You see African-American history does not begin with slavery. It runs deep and far and represents is the ancient history that the entire world seeks to claim as its own.

If we were to explore African-American contribution to the American culture, you will see elements of our historical influence for we are an ancient people. There are African cultural elements and language weaved within American society and even Christian worship.

From a linguistic point of view: the use of the word "massa", an alleged mispronunciation by southern slaves of the word "master", was used to mischaracterize slaves as being illiterate. In actuality, for the majority of slaves, it was far from the truth. Even today you need not travel but as far as the state of Mississippi to visit historical slave quarters and you will see slave writings in Arabic, a language that is most complex and difficult to speak much less write but to many slaves this was their written language. This is evidence that they were not illiterate but perhaps they just didn't speak English.

Massa is in fact the correct Bainouk and Cassanga ethnic group pronunciation of Mansa, the word used by the Mande or more specifically the Mandinka peoples in northern and coastal west Africa that means boss or king. It is a mandification of the English language, if you will.

Mande music, prayer, and storytelling also are evident in the descendants of Slaves, specifically to be found in the Gullah people of South Carolina and Georgia – major territories for the intake of African slaves. We pronounce the "for" as "fo" just like our Mandinka ancestors.

African words are a part of the English language such as the word "kunu" meaning boat; "tote" meaning to carry or lift; "yam" meaning sweet potato; "bu bu" meaning a wound. Our ancestors have influenced the English language and have influenced its culture. We are a great people and possess great power, wisdom, and knowledge. America is only as great as the measure of our contribution to it!

Here's another element that will make you say "hmmm". From a religious perspective, even in today's Baptist and Charismatic Christian Churches you will see African influence! When we worship; we dance as though filled with the spirit; stomping our feet just like our ancestors did when in worship in the motherland. We do so without knowing that our ancestors did the same with the understanding that they danced with their feet always touching the ground because they believed the spirit of their ancestors are interred in the ground and when they worship in this manner they made contact with their ancestors who would lead them and guide them through their journey through life. Remember earlier, I wrote that for Africans their ancestors were the original owners of the land and even after death they are believed to be overseers of it, contributing to it harvests continually. We worship in today's Christian churches through dance, just as did our ancestors, not knowing that we are really worshipping the ancestors before us that are interred in the ground. We are asking them to look over us and look over our land through we are all tied!

The content from a letter written in 1755 by Henry Laurens, a founding father and leader of colonial South Carolina states:

the slaves from the River Gambia are preferred to all others with us save from the Gold Coast." He goes on to write: *"Gambians were .... Tall, strong and very dark. Sengalese were considered most intelligent and esteemed for domestic service. Mandingoes were gentle in demeanor but sinking under fatigue."*

This letter, in my opinion, helps to dispel the myth that African slaves and subsequently their descendants were all illiterate, unskilled workers but they were just the opposite, skilled, intelligent and well versed in the arts, agriculture and intellect.

Your history does not begin with slavery! You are a from a civilized, innovative, resourceful, rich and beautiful culture! No longer should there be a need to wear a mask that does not fit us! We should adopt, if any, the masks that signify our great heritage! We are descendants of the original people! Their mask is a mask of honor!

CHAPTER 7

A Spiritual Praise Break! "You Will Live and NOT Die!"

>» ——————— «<

Acts 9:36 – 40

We enter this text where the establishment of the New Testament church is in full swing! The Holy Ghost has descended on those tarrying in the upper room of Jerusalem. The Church governing body had been laid with the establishment of the Deacons. The seeds for the church international had been set by the Apostle Philip witnessing to the Ethiopian eunuch! And even the chief persecutor of the Jews, Saul is now Paul haven't been knocked off his beast and now come to know Jesus! All of this has happened on the heels of Jesus' last recorded words of the Gospel text, of which we have come to know as the Great Commission, that says "Ye shall be witnesses unto me both in Jerusalem, and in all Judea, and in Samaria, and unto the uttermost part of the earth".

In the text, you find Dorcas (also called Tabitha) active in her calling as a servant of the Most High, having ministered to the widows by making garments for them. Dorcas, while well at work in her ministry fell sick and died! Right in the middle of during the work of God! Right in the middle of doing the right things tragedy happens! This brings to mind the age-old question, why do bad things happen to good people! Yet, the text does not pause to address this question but instead it moves on quickly with a steadfast purpose! You see it does not pause to answer the question of why because no matter what question we have, no matter what tragedy we face, God and God alone is the answer!

As we proceed the reader's eyes cannot help but be drawn to the mention of her name! Her name is mentioned twice, once in Hebrew and once in Greek but that does not matter because the meaning is still the same! Her name in either language means beauty and grace. Beauty and grace speak to her demeaner as well as her spiritual acumen! But in the text, her name is quickly connected to her works!

It is significant that she is identified by not just her name but she is also identified by her works! The bible says the widows were standing by showing the many garments and coats that the deceased had made them! They were aware of her death but they were fixated on what she had done for them while she was alive. When they thought of her works, they remembered her name! Her name is connected to her works! You see a good name is more desirable than great riches! You read nothing of a husband! You hear nothing of how many kids she had! You don't know whether she has any surviving family members but she is only identified is by her name and her good works!

There are many out there today that have a recognizable name but it is tied to unrighteousness! There are many out there today that have a famous name but it is tied to sexual immorality! There are many out there that have their name in lights but it is tied to corruption! There are many out there that have a name but it is tied to lewdness, pain and despair!

The bible says that Dorcas served the Lord with all of heart and her name is connected to righteousness! Her name is connected to beauty! Her name is connected to grace! A good name is worth more than riches! Blesseth are they that die in the Lord; for they rest from their labor and their works will follow them!

Dorcas was a symbol of service and a conduit of Grace to the community but then this grace suddenly dies! What do you do when the Grace that is over your life suddenly and seemingly dies? What do you do when you feel the grace over your life is drying up? The bible indicates that they put their minds on rewind! They recalled the testimonies of Jesus raising Lazarus from the dead! They recalled how Jesus touched the coffin of the widow at Nain and restored her son! They fixed their minds on the one who they thought was dead yet lives! They recalled Jesus saying greater works will you do because I go to my Father! When the Grace over your life feels as though it is drying up! You've got to put your minds on remind and recall what the Lord has done for you! He woke you up this morning with activity in your limbs! He woke you up this morning with a praise on your lips! He woke you up this morning with the strength to lift up Holy hands! He didn't let you die in your sleep but he caused you to awake with worship on your mind!

You may have felt like you were going to die right in the middle of your ministry! You might have thought you were going to die before you saw old age! You might have felt that you were going to die in the middle of your purpose but I've got good news for you today! God is not through with you yet! Don't give up on God! God will never give up on you!

The scripture says, after her death, they take her not to the grave; they didn't hurry up and bury her! These are people of Faith! The text says they washed her body and then they took her to the upper room (indicating a place where they could talk to God)! You see the location of where you take your problem is of utmost importance!

They didn't take her to the grave! Cause some people try to bury you too soon! They give up on you too soon! They are trying to get rid of you quickly because they want what you have for themselves! The bible says that they didn't take her to the grave! The bible says they took her to the upper room! They took her to the upper room! They didn't see death as the end! They took her to the upper room! The upper room is the place where they knew they could connect with God! They took her to the place where they knew they could meet God! When you are in despair! If you feel like you've overwhelmed with problems, you've got to know where to take your cares; your grief! You've got to take them to the upper room! You've got to take them to Jesus! Jesus will fix it! You will live and not die!

You must understand the context of this scripture! In order to understand the full gravity of this text, you must understand that at this point 2/3 of the New Testament scripture had not been written. Paul, who would eventually become the Apostle Paul, though converted was yet to mature in the gospel! He was yet to be the Paul that was a ready writer of the book of Romans and Corinthians; Galatians and Ephesians, Philippians and Colossians and so on. There was limited written scripture that the people of Joppa had to stand on at that time! So that had to stand on what they had!

You find the Believers of this era standing on their testimonies! They were standing on the testimonies of those that first saw Jesus alive after a very real death! They were standing on the testimonies of the Apostle Thomas' who doubted the Resurrection of Jesus until he touched the nail scars on Jesus' hands for himself and felt the scarred piercing of His side! They were standing by Faith! Faith endures trials! Faith understands temptations! Faith obeys the Word! Faith produces action! Faith responds to the promises of God! They were walking by Faith and not by sight! And it is this faith that drove them to the upper room! While they take her to the upper room the Lord dropped in their spirit that the Apostle Peter was in the neighborhood!

Don't you know that God will give you a right now Word for whatever you are going through!!!! God gives the disciples a right now Word and the Word is to call for Peter; he is in the neighborhood! Peter is in the neighborhood! Call for Peter and tell him to "Come immediately!" As soon as Peter gets the word, he makes haste to come at their word!

Now if I can sidebar here for just a second! The bible says that Peter made haste! Now this is the new Peter; the converted Peter! You couldn't have called on Peter when he was known as Simon (the shaky one) he might not have shown up! But now is the perfect timing! It's God's timing! They call for a converted, Holy Ghost filled, fire baptized Peter who is now known as the Rock! The dependable one! When they call on the Rock; the Rock didn't hesitate to show up! You must know as a believer that when you call on the Rock! When you call on Him! He will show up! My bible says that He is a very present Help in the time of trouble! The name of the Lord is a strong tower and the righteous run thereto and are saved! You've got to call on him when you need him! You've got to call on Him the bad times! You've got to call on Him in the turbulent times! You've got to call on Him in the good times!!! You have got to call on HIM! In this text Jesus shows up in the person of Peter! He can show up in you just like He showed up in Peter!

Peter gets to the upper room and when he gets there, he assesses the situation and what he discerns is that the atmosphere is not conducive for faith to work!! There is fear in the room! God does not give us a spirit of fear but of love! There is grief in the room! The faith of some is not strong in the room! We know this because even though they are in the upper room to connect with God they are still holding on to what was and not what will be! The text says they are showing the coats Dorcas made them as though it was the end of her story! They are showing the garments Dorcas knitted and holding on to them as though death had the last word but death does not have the last word God does!

Peter immediately puts them out of the room! You've got to surround yourself with a Faithful atmosphere! You've got to have Faithful surroundings! You can't have people around you that don't have the same level of faith you have! You've got to put them out! Love on them but put them out! Hug on them but put them out! Pray for them later but put them out! Your life depends on it! Jesus is ready to save now! You've got to put them out! Jesus is ready to heal now! You've got to put them out! Jesus is ready to bless now! Jesus is ready to make you whole now! Put them out! Jesus is ready to deliver now!

Take sin out of your life! Put out despair in your life! Put out trouble in your life! Put out distractions in your life! Jesus is ready now! Jesus says behold, I stand at the door and knock if any man hears my voice and open the door, I will come in to him, and will sup with him and he with me!

Peter is in the neighborhood now! God is in the neighborhood now! It happens that Peter before time was in Lydda visiting one name Aeneaus who too had been bedridden for 8 years with the palsy! Peter says to him "Aenaeaus! Jesus Christ maketh thee whole! Arise and make thy bed!!! Likewise, Peter calls out to Tabitha (Dorcas)! Tabitha (Dorcas) arise!

Dorcas opened her eyes: she saw Peter, she sat up! And that is the message! When you see Jesus, you will sit up! When you see Jesus, you will rise up! When you let Him work fully in your life you will Step up! You will step up to greatness! Step up to righteousness! Step up to Holiness! Step up to Joy! Step up to Peace! Step up in Faith! When you see Jesus, you will rise up! Weeping may endure for a season but joy cometh in the morning! Don't give up on God for He won't give up on you!

He didn't give up when they hung Him high! He didn't give up when they stretched him wide! He hung his head for us He died!!!! Don't give up on God! God is able to do just what he said he would do! He's going to fulfill every promise! He will do exceedingly, abundantly above all you could ask, according to the power that worketh in you! Don't give up on Him! God Can and God Will take care of you!

CHAPTER 8

Sankofa: A Change of Direction

»» ———————————— ««

They've told your story for far too long! It's time to rewrite the script! Time to tell your story and not his story! In fact, it's time to rewrite the script and tell the whole story from our perspective! One that is true to us and reveals who we really are!

It is easy to find and learn of the stories of reckless, criminal behavior of black men. Although this has been pervasive, due to the various reasons aforementioned, it does not paint the entire picture of black men! It does not tell the whole story! It is time to tell the stories of many single men and single women who have had kids out of wedlock and did not finish high school or obtained a secondary degree! However, many of these same men and women have gone on to achieve mighty exploits. Many are now PhD's, MD's, Nurses, Entrepreneurs! Many, though they have criminal records, they did not let that define them! They overcame and have achieved unsurmountable feats! We all can do the same!

Time to change your direction and walk into your greatness! Time to take your destiny in your own hand! Time to manage your tomorrow for it is the beginning of a great future! Managing our tomorrow and taking our destiny into our own hands will usher in a change for this country. However, in order to change the very direction of this country, in fact, in order to take our destiny into our own hands we must first be reconciled to our past! We must seek and find both a spiritual healing, mental healing and an emotional healing which will allow us to no longer wear the mask of protection; the mask of defense!

Unless we come to the understanding that we are somebody and that God made us fearlessly and wonderfully; there is no mistake in who we are! We have purpose! It is not until we remove the mask and face the fact that no one can be a better us than us. You are enough and you are a valuable asset to society and to this world!

We are responsible for the removal of the invisible mask we were and not anyone else! We have to change our direction! We have to take our destiny in our own hands! We are responsible for managing our tomorrow and making our future great!

I believe a major part of the change of direction is education! Education (or vocational training whatever your choice) will enable us to establish autonomy. It will allow us to establish our own Black Wall Streets (again). It will allow us to build wealth that pass down! Now is the time to strike out and take everything they said you couldn't have and what has previously been denied of you! from generation to generation! It will empower you and propel you closer to greatness! It first starts now and it starts with us!

Education is empowering, and can be a powerful means of empowering the dis-empowered. It can be an indispensable weapon that can be used to fight against and overcome racism and discrimination. Education is a powerful force that can be used to turn around the devastation and socio-economic disparity seen in the African American families and their communities. Education is power and the key to turning around socio-economic disparity in our communities and to re-instituting the African male into his central role in the family and community.

Education must be undertaken with the understanding that we must educate to successfully integrate into society—to become an integral part of it. We must use education as a platform from which our gifts and talents can be launched and used for the betterment of society. We must be use education wisely that we might integrate into society and not merely assimilate to the norms of society, for assimilation merely smothers our gifts and talents. It causes us to lose our identities, and not to use our very uniqueness and diversity to broader the horizons and hopes of this world. We therefore must be careful to educate, to integrate, and not assimilate.

Looking closer at education and the method of educating, I have come to realize that very little thought has been given to the method of education that one undergoes. From early childhood to adulthood, what we have been exposed to, what we have overheard, and what we have been taught institutionally has shaped who we are. The method of exposure or learning undoubtedly has contributed much to our learning capabilities, and as such, has shaped the way we learn. Considering this, it would be safe to conclude that the systems in which we have acquired education can either mold an individual in the way of oppression (in a way that does not give the individual the opportunity to use his/her unique gifts and talents), or position an individual towards liberation. In either case, the power of education is expressed and the method in which it is introduced can become the catalyst for change or assimilation. I'd like to share as a means of re-enforcing and bringing clarity to my point, my attitude and experience with education. Below is a bit of my story. I hope it helps!

Throughout my life, I have been constantly challenged by adversity, and through its friendships were born. One friend of which I speak is education, and the mother of it has been oppressive social injustice of the rural south.

Having grown up in rural Mississippi in the sixties, I am no stranger to adversity. Hangings of colored people either for sport or because they were rebels to the status quo, was a mainstay in Mississippi during this time. Invisible lines of demarcation traversed the geography. If you were colored, you knew your place. Regardless of age, every white person was to be referred to as "Yes Sir" or "Yes Ma'am," depending upon the gender of course. The entire landscape of the South was painted with oppression; everything was either black or white, no gray. If you were white, you were right, wealthy, intelligent, and privileged. The entire world belonged to you. If you were black (or in the vernacular of the time, colored) you were the lowest of the lowest. You were incapable of learning. You were the ethnos, the other ones, and were not to mix with the esteemed social class of the time.

As one might imagine, an environment such as the one previously depicted was one swollen with tension, even the air that a colored person breathed seemed to be rationed. Something had to change if we were to go on living. We could no longer be ignored. The efforts of Malcolm X, Martin Luther King, and the likes, demanded that the oppressive discriminatory practices so prevalent in the rural south could no longer be ignored. Some of the offspring of attempts to stabilize and neutralize the south were integration and bussing.

I was totally adjusted in my classroom. The environment was very comfortable. I had colored teachers. There were colored students. I had colored friends. My environment was a utopia. Then one day we are all separated, bussed in a manner that was reminiscent of the transatlantic slave trade, to an all-white institution twenty miles in the opposite direction of where I was accustomed. Thoughts ravished my mind: "What did we do wrong?"; "Why did I have to leave my friends?" etc. We were thrust right into the middle of chaos. The white students didn't want us there and we didn't want to be there. Interracial fighting became the norm. We were in the midst of integration and it wasn't going smoothly. Day after day, the occurrences were the same and there was no hope of any change. We were there to stay, so we had better make the best of it. I settled in and began to focus intently on my studies, ignoring all that was around me. Integration and bussing had taught me to accept that which I seemingly had no power to control. A lesson that in some way, shape, or form remains with me over forty years later. Adversity was beginning to have labor pains.

I remained in my one-dimensional, educational, mental tunnel all through high school. I had learned that regardless of what was going on around me, the task still needed to be completed. As a result, I performed well academically. I was able to spew out exactly what my teachers wanted me to. I had become a recorder, able to play back all that I had heard because of the unwillingness to think critically. In fact, I was also afraid, believing that chaos would ensue again if I challenged the status quo.

I graduated in the top ten of my class in an all predominately white institution. At graduation, I heard all of the white students, practically all below me academically, being announced as having received scholarships to this college or to that college. I became confused. I questioned what was going on (in my mind of course). I had better grades. Why wasn't I offered academic scholarships to any colleges? I soon discovered that the school guidance counselor had not counseled me at all. I was left to go it alone. I was number thirteen of fifteen kids, and none before me had ever attended college. I had no road map, no blueprint to follow. I had to do it myself. I couldn't trust anyone to help me. I was being educated to go it alone. Adversity's contractions were getting stronger.

After high school graduation, I took some time to reflect. I looked back over my life, considering all that I had been exposed to and had overcome. I looked at my brothers' and my sisters' consideration of choices they had made regarding life. I looked at my family as a whole and assessed that, although we were not very well educated, we were a very talented family. Nevertheless, we remained in poverty. I looked at my white counterparts drawing upon their academic efforts while in high school, and quickly discerned that I saw no difference between them and us (besides skin color). I recognized that college was not an option for them. It was mandatory. It was then that I began to experience fear, a new type of fear. This fear was the fear of remaining in poverty, constantly being victimized by the oppressive discriminatory practices of the rural south. I realized that I had to do something different. Devoid of a blueprint, I reached for that which seemed obvious. I would attempt to mirror the steps of my white counterparts. I was to assimilate.

I enrolled in a ninety-seven percent white college. I was to dress the part (as best as I could afford). I was to speak their language. I was to be seen as non-threatening in an attempt to penetrate their civic organizations. I was to be all that they required of me and I succeeded (so I thought). It wasn't until I was about to graduate that I began to realize that assimilation was not only uncomfortable to me, but it represented betrayal to all that had labored before me. The goal of those that had paved the way for the black race was for us to contribute to bettering our race as a whole, not to lose sight of and dishonor it by assimilating.

These reflections took on life for me when one of my professors informed me that she was going to change one of my grades from a B to an A, for seemingly no reason at all. I began to think that if she was going to do that now, how many times will she do it in the negative direction throughout my stay at the university. I had another similar incident when my advisor (of the white race) attempted very strongly to get me to reconsider my plans to go to a predominately black college to pursue graduate work. His reasoning, although he assured me that he was looking out for my best interest, appeared to me as though he had a problem with Historically Black Institutions. I quickly realized that assimilation had not liberated me. I was still trapped below the hull of oppression and discrimination. Again, I was facing adversity and her contractions were getting intense.

I had achieved a milestone for my family. I was the first to graduate from college. Unsure of what I was going to do with the degree I obtained, I decided to work during the summer on the farm with my dad. It was this experience that was to throw me for a total loop. We were assigned (my dad and I and a few others) to spray all of the cotton plants in the fields with pesticide in order to rid the crop of weeds. After working for some time, we were out of pesticide and decided and to take the long walk back to the shop where we were to ask the supervisor (a white man) to refuel our vessels. However, when we got there he was nowhere to be found. In an attempt to remedy the situation, I walked over to the bottle of concentrated pesticide, read the directions for dilution, and proceeded to dilute the product. It was then that screams bombarded my ears. Stop!!!! Don't do it! Startled, I froze and looked at my father and the other workers with amazement. My amazement quickly turned to disgust, and I realized that the only way to get out of this oppression was through education. I had to totally thrust myself into education in an attempt to liberate my family from this oppressive regime. A friend had been birthed through adversity and that friend was education.

Indeed, a friend is born out of adversity. Adversity in my life had become the stimulus through which I was to achieve liberation for my family. No longer were we to be victims of the oppressive discriminatory regime of the rural south. Education was to be the tool through which we were to escape poverty. Education was to be the weapon that we were to use to destroy the victimization brought about through discrimination and social injustice. Adversity had indeed shaped the way I lived my life. It had shaped the way I viewed every situation. Adversity had birthed in me the desire to acquire knowledge. I was to approach education with an attitude that no one was going to help me achieve anything. I had to do it alone. I was to block out all distractions around me and focus on the task at hand, while at the same time maintaining my ethnicity and my identity that had been shaped by my black experience. Liberation had screamed without the chained doors of adversity, and I embraced education as my friend.

Education has allowed me to contribute to my family and to my community. The experiences that I have gained over the years, I have shared with them, and as a result, many who might not have attended college or gained further education have done so. Education has raised the socio-economic level of my family from below poverty level to above it, and all that have tasted the fruit of it have maintained their identities and have contributed to those who have come behind them. Our communities are on the rise. It is a work in progress, and I believe that as we continue to educate, we will reach great heights as a people and as a nation. We will re-establish our family ties to the point of old, and we will rebuild our communities so that they may flourish the way God had intended them. They will be safe havens to all who choose to come within their borders, and will owe it all to education, which is the great equalizer and friend to all who choose to embrace it. It is a means of achieving Sankofa—a change in direction that will lead to you to self-empowerment, self-authentication and self-love! Mask-free!

CHAPTER 9

Time for Healing

As we have learned thus far, the African American male, as a result of family and community dysfunctionality and systematic exclusion, has deteriorated to a point where the values, ethics, beliefs and high esteem that were evident within his past legacy are no longer evident. He is yet a fraction of what his ancestors were, and what God has created him to be.

Due to dysfunctionality of the African American family and their communities, the African African males' identity has been lost and his net worth lessened. Yet, if we were to poll the racial majority group within this country, they would say that "everything is find just the way they are". They would say that the progress that was made during the civil rights error was sufficient to allow minorities to function at an acceptable level within society. Jawanza Kunjufu in his book entitled *Black Economics, Solutions for Economic and Community Empowerment* (African American Images, 1991) states: "The issue of civil rights had been a major public concern in the mid-1960s, but it has been declining in popularity for the past 25 years. Surveys show that Whites believe that the problems have been solved…"

In the eyes of the majority some gains without equal status within society is enough for the minority group. Small gains are enough to satisfy the conscience of the descendants of slave owners, and not convict them of the travesty of their past. But for the victimized, it is only an offer of a greater hope that seems to escape them. This offering of little hope frustrates the victimized because it reaggravates wounds that have been slightly healed. It can be compared to putting a band aide over a deep gash in one's heart.

The psyche, soul and heart of the African American male need healing. Every measure to date has been an attempt to fix the social problems working in today's society. The Civil Rights Movement's focus was equal rights! The Back to Africa Movement belief was that the cultures of the majority and minority couldn't coexist. Affirmative Action, although necessary, was an attempt to fix the problem of discrimination. If we are to exist as one nation working together to achieve and promote the American ideals of liberty and justice for all, then we must do more than attempt to fix the problems that afflict its people. We must develop measures, programs and methods that seek to heal the wounds of our past, not simply fix them.

The approach must be therapeutic and not punitive. It must not create emotional unhealthiness in one group, while creating health for the other. The approach cannot offer opportunity for one, while disenfranchising the other. The approach has to be one that works towards the universal good, one that celebrates the unique yet diverse gifts and talents of all that live within its borders.

I believe the measures that we take as a group and as a nation must begin at the simplest level, which is the family. We must work to heal the family and the community. In order to do so, we must understand the dynamics of each individual ethnic group's family. Once we understand, that the African

American male's very identity is tied to his family and community, we then can create measures that uniquely address the ills of the African American family. If this approach is applied to every ethnic group, the result will be the saving of our communities and our nation. We will achieve moral victory, which is a victory that is more everlasting than any judicial or legislative system could ever hope to achieve.

In the biblical book of Malachi 4:6, the Lord makes aware the condition of the family during the prophet's time. There was a breakdown in the family, and it was having a devastating impact on the Israelite community. In this passage, the Lord provides the solution to the problem at hand. He simply declares that before the world comes to an end, I will turn the hearts of the fathers to the children, and the hearts of the children to their fathers, and if I don't the devastation will get worse.

Malachi 4:6 (KJV)

"Behold, I will send you Elijah the prophet before the coming of the great and dreadful day of the Lord. And he will turn the hearts of the fathers to the children, and the hearts of the children to their fathers, lest I come and strike the earth with a curse."

As we can see from the text, God delineates the importance of family and its contribution to a positive community. In my mind and in my heart, there is nothing greater than what God says about a matter. Therefore, the solution to the ills affecting the African American male and his family and community, is to provide healing to the hearts of the fathers and children, i.e. the family. Once we achieve this, the healing will begin to take place! Once we develop and implement measures that integrate and restore the African American male to his rightful place within his family and community, then it will have an effect that will be transforming to not only his community, but to the nation.

The solution for a better society and a better way is to ensure that we promote healing within those who have been disenfranchised, discriminated against, expelled, excluded, and raped of their net worth. We must promote healing and not fixing, if we are to save our families and communities. We are in need of real change, and that change can only come through healing of wounds that drive us towards being a better group of people.

CHAPTER 10

Undiagnosed PTSD

»» ———————— ««

Too often, we see an individual demonstrating destructive behavior either towards themselves or towards someone else. Traditional thought and response to such behavior would result in attributing blame to the individual observed demonstrating the behavior. The natural verbal response or conscious thought elicited would probably be something like, *"what's his problem?"* Due to social construction, we often take a *"point the finger"* or *"place the blame"* approach to every situation that does not fit neatly into what we feel is normal or acceptable in our world. Rarely, do we stop to think beyond what he/she has observed. We, for whatever reason, choose not to consider the action any further, and in so doing, we label the person observed solely as the victimizer when quite possibly they might be both the *victimizer and victimized.*

I'd like to share a childhood story with you, if I may. Growing up in the rural South, engulfed in oppressive systemic racial discrimination, I have experienced many hardships. I have experienced personally the right hook of a segregated South that strikes with evil intent those not a part of the socio-economic majority. I have watched with my very eyes, the arm of injustice reaches out with crippling fervor to pull the legs out from under those who, with their very arms, once held them as though a mother weaning her newborn child. I have watched with perplexity, the feet of southern power structure stomp the face and body of those who looked kindly on them, the ones who used their God-given bodies to farm land that was once theirs, but now taken away from them. These are the emotional scars of an oppressive South within whose borders I grew up, the memories of which I would like to share briefly with you.

I recall first hand, in the early seventies, being bused from an all-black (pardon me, the nomenclature of the time branded us colored), all colored school twenty-five miles in the opposite direction of the colored school, in which I had attended from my home. This was done all in the name of integration, and was the result of the Civil Rights Movement that was designed to make the world a better place.

These times were hard! I remember the first day at this all white school. My brother, one of my sisters and I, got off the now integrated bus, having withstood the stares and grimaces of those that resisted change. I was seven at the time, my brother was nine, and my sister was eight. We stepped off the bus and made our way to our respective classes. The day went relatively smooth, but it was the ride home that was to mark this day, a day that would be etched in my mind and the minds of my siblings forever.

On the way home, my brother and sister did not expect the ride home to be any different than the ride to school that morning. However, little did we know that while we were riding, one of the older white boys on the bus began calling us names and shouting expletives. The atmosphere on the bus had changed from the stares and grimaces we faced on the ride to school, to one of hostility. One of the older white boys decided to take aggressive action against my slightly older brother. The white boy was about sixteen or so and my brother was only nine. The white boy attacked my brother, as my sister and I watched, unable to do or say anything for we were paralyzed by shock. Undoubtedly fueled by socially constructed uncontrolled racial hatred towards blacks and the fear of social change, the white boy stomped my brother's face with combat boots, and continued to stomp him. Blood was everywhere! The bus driver, a white person, didn't react to the beating at all. He/she (as I can't remember the gender of the driver) just kept driving as though nothing was happening. I couldn't continue to look. I was helpless, scared, and traumatized. I turned my face to the back of the bus until the attack was over. The attack didn't cease until the driver came to the house of the older white boy that was doing the beating. I caught another glimpse of the attacker after hearing the driver wish him a good afternoon, and seeing him through the bus rear window as we drove off. My brother lifted himself off of the bus floor in silence and just sat there until we arrived home.

As we arrived home, my mother and father were astonished. They didn't know what to do! That night, I heard my older sisters and brothers planning to resolve the situation on the next morning. I had twelve brothers and sisters enrolled in school at that time, and they were very protective of their younger siblings. They had planned to resolve the situation with violence. I listened intently, taking it all in and meditating on it throughout the night. Little did I know, my soul was being imprinted, my emotional well-being was being scarred, and my life was entering a stage of fragmentation, due to the painful events that had transpired and that had set off a dangerously vicious pattern of violence that a young seven year old, or any adolescent for that matter, would have difficulty rebounding from. We were products of the time; victims of a cruel society that was bent on resisting change, and unless emotional help lie somewhere in the future, life was to be filled with internal struggles that would not complicate our lives, but those of our not-to-distant families.

The next morning all of my brothers and sisters boarded the bus. Everyone was waiting for the older white boy, who attacked my brother, to board but he never did. His father had taken him to school that day in fear of retaliation. His father was trying to protect him. Well, that didn't stop my brothers and sisters. When the bus arrived at the now integrated school, one of my siblings recognized the boy from a distance and all of my siblings ran after him. The boy ran into the principal's office hoping to find protection, but that didn't help. That day, the boy and the principal all suffered at the hands of my siblings. The method of corporate nonviolent social change had developed within it a Malcolm Xism. The nonviolent social change movement of the time had resulted in integration of the schools, but a "by any means necessary" method had resolved an attack of violence perpetrated against a helpless colored child, by a white adolescent socially conditioned for racial hatred.

Because of this incident, the family—my brother in particular—were never the same. We all remember it like it was yesterday. My brother, the victim of the violence is now emotionally scared. He is outraged when anyone, white, black, brown, or yellow, according to his perception, tries to undermine or invade his personal space. He has spent a lifetime trying to adjust to those who run big business. He has spent a lifetime trying to establish himself as a positive contributor to society, and now being a father, he has tried hard to raise his children in a way that moves them towards emotional wholeness, all the while, holding in memory the painful past of his childhood. He never received counseling. He never received any psychotherapy. He simply repressed the pain, as did I. We simply locked the incident away in the deep, dark crevices of our mind, only to visit them occasionally, but to have them played out continually within our personal lives. We were victimized that day, and because of that victimization, we became victimizers. I am not condoning our behavior, but what I am saying is that sometimes you can't know the reason for destructive behavior just by observing it. You must know the history of the person exhibiting that behavior, and if you care enough seek to get an understanding, for you never know God might want to use you to bring about healing in their lives. Let's not *point the finger* or merely *assign blame*! Let's seek to understand!

This *"point the finger"* or *"place the blame"* does not open pathways for understanding behavior, it merely assigns blame, all the while leaving the person demonstrating the negative behavior, to continue that behavior uncorrected. The approach of assigning blame merely seeks to categorize behavior. After all, we exist in a world that cannot function unless it assigns labels.

Diverse groups of people cannot exist solely as diverse members of the human race because society must place a label on their diversity. Blacks must be labeled as one thing; whites must be labeled as another thing and so forth. Our preoccupation with labels obstructs our ability to comprehend the larger problem. It stops progress before it ever begins; never giving the *victimizer/victimized* an opportunity to be understood. In the end we write the individual off, and they eventually end up trapped in our criminal justice system, rarely finding their way back into mainstream society. As we all should know, our criminal justice system is not a fix. It is merely a holding cell system where the unwanted, disenfranchised, misunderstood and disavowed are kept, so that mainstream America may live in a false sense of security. We are all called to do something greater for all humankind! We are to not simply cast blame, but work together to help our fellow brethren, and to heal the wounds of the *victimizer/victimized* that he might be re-acclimated into the community.

I am not suggesting that one should try to understand and subsequently attempt to fix every problem or every negative behavior. But what I am suggesting is that we not be so quick to pass judgment, without first really finding the underlying cause of the behavior, for understanding opens the pathways towards healing.

Renown psychiatrist Murray Bowen presents an interesting methodology for assessing family dynamics, and the stresses present in them. Bowen suggests in his family systems theory that individuals cannot be understood in isolation from one another, but rather as a part of their family, as the family is an emotional unit (Kerr and Bowen 1988). Can you imagine the implications this theory has when placed upon the African American male?

As was stated earlier, the African American males' belief system is one that is rooted within the functional family. Family, to the descendants of African slaves, is more than just the immediate family; it is the community. Therefore, if we apply Bowen's family systems theory to the dysfunctional behavior that presently exists within the African American family, we have a means for examining and understanding their behavior. In doing so, we will be able to develop solutions to the problems affecting them rather than merely assigning blame.

Using the family systems theory to understand the dynamics of African American men provides us with a measure of the devastating impact that slavery, institutionalization, disenfranchisement as well as racial discrimination has had on them. Using this theory, one can begin to understand that what may be driving the imbalance in incarceration rates, test scores, graduation rate, etc., is not the ineptness of the individual in most cases but the social pressures and unfairness that has been pressing in on them since childhood. Racial discrimination, slavery, disenfranchisement, and all of the unfairness imposed upon the African American male, may just well be the root cause of destructive behavior, low self-esteem and family dysfunctionality demonstrated within the African American family. The negative images of African Americans is merely the signal that something is wrong within the family structure, and his acting out is a cry for help!

If we were to change this political/social view to a religious/spiritual view, this notion of identifying the cause not the problem can be better understood if we explicate the passage of scripture found in the gospel of Mark chapter 5 that deals with the demon-possessed man.

Mark 5:1-15;18-20 (King James Version)

1. They went across the lake to the region of the Gerasenes.

2. When Jesus got out of the boat, a man with an evil spirit came from the tombs to meet him.

3. This man lived in the tombs, and no one could bind him anymore, not even with a chain.

4. For he had often been chained hand and foot, but he tore the chains apart and broke the irons on his feet. No one was strong enough to subdue him.

5. Night and day among the tombs and in the hills he would cry out and cut himself with stones.

6. When he saw Jesus from a distance, he ran and fell on his knees in front of him.

7. He shouted at the top of his voice, "What do you want with me, Jesus, Son of the Most High God? Swear to God that you won't torture me!"

8. For Jesus had said to him, "Come out of this man, you evil spirit!"

9. Then Jesus asked him, "What is your name?"

10. "My name is Legion," he replied, "for we are many."

11. And he begged Jesus again and again not to send them out of the area.

12. A large herd of pigs was feeding on the nearby hillside.

13. The demons begged Jesus, "Send us among the pigs; allow us to go into them."

14. He gave them permission, and the evil spirits came out and went into the pigs. The herd, about two thousand in number, rushed down the steep bank into the lake and were drowned.

15. Those tending the pigs ran off and reported this in the town and countryside, and the people went out to see what had happened.

16. When they came to Jesus, they saw the man who had been possessed by the legion of demons, sitting there, dressed and in his right mind; and they were afraid.

17. As Jesus was getting into the boat, the man who had been demon-possessed begged to go with him.

18. Jesus did not let him, but said, "Go home to your family and tell them how much the Lord has done for you, and how he has had mercy on you."

19. So the man went away and began to tell in the Decapolis how much Jesus had done for him. And all the people were amazed.

In this text, we have a man who has been disenfranchised by his community and is now confined to live outside of it in the tombs. The man was viewed by others as a menace. He was thought of as being a problem, and no one took his cries or his fighting as attempts to overcome that which had removed him from society. They only took him to be a menace!

It is not until the end of the passage that we come to realize that this man had a family and he had friends. Nevertheless, no one stopped to understand what was the reason why he was separated from his friends, family, and community. They only tucked him neatly away from society, incarcerated without any immediate remedy for that which ailed him, that is until Jesus came on the scene. The man recognized the solution to the thing(s) that vexed him and took it into his own hands to receive his healing. He broke from the chains that bound him and fell at the feet of salvation—Jesus! Jesus rebuked that which vexed the man and restored him to his friends, family and community!

We see from this text that Jesus was fully aware of the family systems theory, long before Bowen articulated it. He recognized that the destructive behavior that the man was eliciting was not the cause of his condition, but merely the signal that something greater was wrong. Jesus addressed the cause, and in so doing, healed the man so that he might rejoin, contribute and become an integral part of his community.

The African American men of today are in a similar state of depravity! They have been so hardened by societal woes that they are detached and disconnected. They have very little feeling towards humankind and are in a state of survival, which drives them to do any and everything to maintain life. Their hearts have been so hardened by the system of institutionalization, that they are now detached from social norms and moral decency. They have been wronged, abandoned, and raped of hope, that they are walking down a road which to them is devoid of hope. They heap up for themselves treasures that are temporary and unfulfilling. Society continues with its daily business relinquishing these individuals to the judicial system, and isolating itself from the reality that we are all created to function in relationship to each another.

I believe, just like Jesus restored the demoniac to his family and community, the African American man can be restored as well. I know, internally there is a voice that is begging for help. They've heard of Jesus, his history, his word of healing and restoration, but they are now waiting for the word to become flesh in their lives. They are not the problem! They are both the *victimizer/victimized*! Trying to understand the cause of their human condition is a better way to address the state of which they are in, and the family system theory relegates dysfunctional behavior not just to the one who is behaving dysfunctionally. It seeks to understand that the one who is acting out is merely the signal that points to a greater problem.

CHAPTER 11

A Method for Obtaining Wholeness

Many people question whether an individual can change his or her behavior. They wonder whether an individual's character traits can really change. These individuals, for whatever reason or another, believe that once a person's personality is constructed at a young age, then it is set for life. This belief that personalities are human constructs is widespread; in fact, many that are highly regarded in the field of academia and research on human behavior support this belief. They underscore this belief when they suggest that by the age of five, a person's personality is constructed. According to Sigmund Freud (a renown psychiatrist and psychoanalyst), we all journey through three stages of personality development, which shapes us for the remainder of our lives. The first stage is the Id (that part of us that allows us to get our needs met). The second stage is the Ego (that part of us that interprets and transfers the reality of every situation and thus keeps in check the Id). The last stage is the Superego (the moral beliefs and ideals that we learn from our parents or caregivers by the age of five). This hypothesis still provides the foundation for how we view human development. Therefore, it is contended that what a person is, and what he or she is predisposed to by age five, shapes his or her personality for the remainder of his life.

We even have certain colloquialisms such as "he's set in his ways", or "you can take the boy out of the country but you can't take the country out of the boy", that serve as verbal attestations to cultural beliefs, which underscore that change in individual personality is highly unlikely and culturally disregarded. These colloquialisms give indication as to how deep the notion of resistance to change is woven into the fabric of American society.

This notion of resistance to behavioral modification that exists among American society, gives rise to many societal complexities that impact a variety of social groups. The belief becomes that all blacks are the same and cannot change; all whites are the same and cannot change, etc. In essence, it gives voice to a nation and culture that is steeped in tradition, making it difficult to move to a society that will equality embrace others.

On the surface, our society professes that change can occur. However, upon close examination, we will find that this profession is only smoke and mirrors. Consider our prison system—termed "correctional facilities". The nomenclature suggests that change of human behavior is plausible. It suggests that our prison system works to correct or change the behavior of those who have demonstrated behavior contrary to the laws of the land. If the incarcerated individual puts his/her time in and follows the rules, then change will occur.

We put millions of dollars into these systems yearly, further lending support that change is possible. While we put millions in support of the system that declares that it can correct behavior, we see no real change in the crime rate (see statistics cited earlier in this work) and an increase in the number of repeat offenders. Correctional facilities—the prison system—are only a façade. Correctional facilities are not a place for positive change. They are merely holding cells, formed to rid society of what they have labeled dysfunctional deviants. The correctional system at work in America is merely a system that underscores our society's resistance to change.

I must say that if we accept the way society has demonstrated its attitude concerning behavior modification, there is not much hope for individuals trapped on the negative end of this social behavior continuum. Individuals who are born in or exposed to particularly non-affirming or negative environments, are, as a consequence, labeled as social misfits with no hopes of changing or ever contributing positively to their families and communities, or to the betterment of themselves. According to society, they are doomed to repeat the same experiences that they have learned from the days of their youth. They are trapped with no choice and with no hope of ever breaking from the chains of their past. They are trapped in a generational cycle of negative behavior.

In fact, our outlook does not provide much hope for anyone seeking to better himself or herself, whether or not they were born into negative environments. Nevertheless, there are individuals out there that embrace diversity—they embrace change—whether its diversity from their family members or friends, diversity from the members of their communities or diversity for the betterment of themselves throughout life. They feel change is inevitable. They feel change is needed. For them, to change is to grow, and growth must occur in order to advance society, in order to better ourselves. Growth must occur or, else, life would cease.

If we ever want our children to achieve greater success than we do, change must be a part of the process. Spiritually speaking, the LORD demonstrated change in the process of human development. The LORD, on one occasion, divested Himself of all of His glory, became as a little babe, born in a manger, and grew in all wisdom and knowledge. He changed before his family's very eyes to become what God preordained him to be, even before the beginning of time. He grew both in wisdom and in knowledge. His personality exhibited as a young child before the age of twelve, was quite different than what the people of his family and community witnessed once he reached twelve. The passage, "Is this not the carpenters' son?" (Matthew 13:55, KJV) provides credence to this change in personality. Therefore, if God exhibited change through the Son, we as His creation should have a similar desire and an attitude of acceptance towards change for, we were created in HIS image.

Now that we have established that there exists within society an attitude of resistance to behavioral modification, how does one who chooses to embrace change succeed in doing so? For the most part, history has shown that individuals that embrace change and have a desire to implement it, believes that sheer will power will do it. We see demonstrations of this belief model year after with the passage of time. Individuals within this belief system make New Year resolutions to change a certain behavior, or resolute to lose weight, or be a nicer person. They work within themselves to achieve the goal of which they have set. Many, if not all of them, will fail at achieving their goal and, as a result, will make the same resolution again before the strike of twelve next New Year's Eve, or they will achieve their goal only to relapse into the same behavior or state they were in. Many will become frustrated and will resolve themselves to believe the notion of resistance to change that makes up the fabric of traditional society. Many will give up, never giving effort to positive change again because they failed at their first attempt. The failure for them becomes a once small hurdle that has become an impossible feat, as one attempting mountain climbing for the first time, and choosing a mountain as tall as Mount Everest as his first endeavor. Obviously, this person is doomed for failure, and unless a plausible intervention occurs, disaster might strike and forever change his/her outlook towards attempting anything great again.

Contrary to popular belief, there is a way to achieve change. There is a way to accomplish whatever change you desire in life. There is a way to become a better father, a better person, a better neighbor, a better husband, a better employee or employer. There is a way to lose weight and keep it off. There is a way to control your emotions. There is a way to overcome addictive behavior! There is a way to becoming whatever you choose to embrace or change within your life.

I'd like to share with you three methods that can be used for embracing change in your life. Three practical principles that, if followed, will help to break the cycle of fallacy that asserts that change is not possible; help you overcome the fear of failing, and move you to becoming a successful, transformed, happier, and positive person. It will provide you with indicators on how to recognize the appropriate environment for change, and how to successfully navigate change within your life. If these principles are embraced with a sense of commitment, if you consistently covenant to continue within these precepts for as long as it takes and then some, you will be able to tackle and change anything within your life. You will be able to take the necessary steps that will carry you to your next horizon in life. You will benefit, your family will benefit, and the world at large will benefit, because you have identified the element that you would like to see happen, by way of tackling it and coming out victorious. Your life will have additional meaning and the cycle of repeating the same old ills of old will have been broken. Together, let's take a walk towards embracing the new you.

For many of us, life has not been easy. We go through a life that is profuse with negative elements that chip away at our sanity; chip away at our emotion stability; and carving elements of pain and resentment into our soul. In order to handle the many traumatic events that we face, we have developed coping mechanisms. Mechanisms like "what doesn't kill you makes you strong;" "boys don't cry;" and even at the child stage of development, we've concocted statements such as "sticks and stones might break my bones but words will never hurt me".

We have developed these proverbial statements, not so much as a declaration of our toughness to society, but as a coping mechanism that help us navigate through the pain that society has caused us. In fact, we use these proverbial statements as a barrier, a wall to keep us insulated from the pain. We merely hide whatever pain there is behind this area of defense, occasionally giving it a glimpse but never outwardly validating it as a source to be reckoned with. As a result, we live our lives fragmented. We go throughout life as a windowpane, containing many cracks but still holding together. We think that no one can see the cracks, but we are a windowpane made of glass and people see right through. At any moment, with just one more devastating blow to the emotional fabric that is struggling to hold us together, we are poised to crack into many tiny pieces, but our resilience holds us together. We are held together by the hope of a better tomorrow.

This discourse paints the picture of the frailty of humankind. It depicts the emotional needs of practically every individual trying to live life. There is a struggle to maintain, and to make safe navigation through the torrential storms of life. Humankind are survivors, and as such, there is an innate ability to ensure self-preservation. We see elements of this throughout our lives. We morph on the surface, taking on chameleon-like attributes in order to continue on the grand scheme of life.

From a psychological perspective, this discourse depicts the need for a deeper change within individuals. It asserts that life inherently will inflict us all with pain, deep emotional stress that play out violent symphonies within the chorus of our emotional being. This discourse underscores as well the human mechanisms inherent to survival.

Humans will create some level of protection, even one that is merely a façade, in order to continue to survive in the game of life, and while this quest for survival is occurring, deep repression of pain and conflict that could very well lead to emotional and physical infirmity is running its course. If there is hope at all, that is hope for wholeness and healing, we must begin to acknowledge our authentic self. We must recognize and call to memory the ills that lie active but conceal within us. Recall is necessary! Recall is a necessary principle that begins the road towards wholeness and emotional, psychological and physical well-being. We must not repress the pain, but embrace it if we are to be the fearfully and wonderfully made creation that God has intended us to be. Recall must be embraced, for it is therapeutic! There is power in remembering. There is a kinetic energy that is released when I outwardly recall the pain of my past, and it is this kinetic energy that acts as the catalyst toward bringing about a change in my physical, emotional, and psychological world. It is like exhaling after holding your breath for decades (if possible).

I exhort you to take a moment of your time to exercise this principle. Try putting this principle into practice. Do it now. Think hard. Pull out those repressed events of your childhood, your adolescent years, or even your adulthood. Don't give up, keep trying. As you focus harder and harder and you begin to remember, you will notice that you might become a little uncomfortable, perhaps even aggravated as you recall the painful events of your past. You have begun to uncover the thing that has been lying concealed within. By doing this exercise, you have begun to identify a source of pain and discomfort.

You'll find that you will attempt to rationalize the events of your past or perhaps even question why it had to happen. You'll say to yourself, "why does life or the world at large have to be so tough?" Perhaps you will even try to justify the painful events of your past. Please note that these grappling is merely the initial stages of healing—the initial stages that must be undertaken if you are to bring about change in your life. Be sure not to give up; this process could take days or even months, but what is important is that you begin to recall the repressed events of your past. Try writing them all down so as to not forget any of them, for they all must be dealt with if you are to achieve the wholeness and emotional wealth that you are predestined to walk in. In addition, be sure to write down your feelings about each of the events that you recall, it will help you to identify things that trigger negative emotions or negative behaviors that attempt to resurface. Remembering and writing things down will help ensure that a definite plan for progress is in place. You will be able to look back at the things that you considered giants in your life, and realize that they were merely small stones that you could have tossed away long ago, by addressing them early and never letting them grow into an illusionary giant that was bent on bullying you and destroying your emotional, psychological and physical health.

In order to bring about change in your life, the principle of reconciliation or coming to terms with your past must be embraced. One must endeavor to bring disturbing events of their past that have been repressed, as a means of protection, to the forefront. It is critical to face the demons of your past, for only in confronting them will you begin to destroy them. You cannot defeat what you are unwilling to confront.

After recalling the repressed feelings and emotions of your past, it is important that you begin to do the opposite of what you've done over the years. Instead of rejecting those feelings and repressing the painful events, it is now time to embrace them. You must now accept them as a part of your life. It must be understood that those experiences, no matter how negative, have served to shape you and make you what you are today. I know they hurt you and I know that it is most difficult to remember them, but ignoring them does not rid you of them. In fact, by ignoring them you are giving them more power over you than they should have. You must bring them forward and begin to make amends with them, for in so doing, they will become less of a hindrance to your progress.

This is a critical step in order to move forward. It can be equated to overcoming the bully that threatened to take your lunch money during your primary school days. What gave power to the bully, his/her robust stature notwithstanding, was their ability to instill fear within their subjects. Think about it! It is the fear that causes a person to behave contrary to the manner that they may want to exhibit. The bully counts on the ones he/she chooses to intimidate to be afraid of them. Once the fear factor is removed, the bully is neutralized. So, it is with the pains of your past. If they remain repressed, they are placed in the position of the bully, unconfronted, they tug, nag, and poke at your peace and freedom. The bully must be dealt with if you are to go on freely with your life. If not, the bully will continue to feed its own ego by the fear that you are demonstrating, and will keep you trapped, unable to fulfill your full potential in life.

When exposed to the threats of a bully or any other negative stimulus, your body's first reaction is one of preparation—preparation to deal with the situation or run from it. In the scientific world, this phenomenon is commonly known as a flight or fight response. When an animal is confronted with a potentially dangerous situation, a series of biological events are initiated. At the point of confrontation, the animal's biological system readies either him/her to confront the source of threat apparent before he/she fights, or having assessed the situation and realizing (remembering) that perhaps he/she is not equipped to deal with the confrontation at the moment, decides to run (flight). The catalyst for behavior in this response system is the biochemical reactions occurring within the animal. These catalysts will elicit a fight response or a flight response. The system will work to eliminate the immediate danger that the animal is confronted with, as a means of protection and survival. However, the fight or flight response was not designed to be a continuous prolonged event. It was designed to be temporary, merely active longer enough to remove the immediate danger or else it will pose a danger to the very thing it was designed to protect.

As is the case of people who have been traumatized, their response to the trauma is dependent upon this same phenomenon. However, in most cases the flight response has been invoked. Most have repressed the event deeply within their subconscious and they refuse to deal with it. For many, the damage inflicted by the trauma has been allowed to linger for years. The traumatic event happened at an age where they simply were not strong enough or mature enough to handle it. Therefore, the only response that they elicited was the flight phenomenon. The flight response that was elicited at such an early age presented itself as a refusal to recall or remember the event, thereby repressing it as a means of protection from the pain. Unfortunately, this repression of the event may have been a necessary response at the time, but the response was not intended to last forever.

The fight or flight response was devised by God to protect us from harm, temporarily. It was not meant to work continuously, uninterrupted throughout our lives. Our systems simply were not designed for it. It you continue to place unwanted and unwarranted stress on a system, ultimately it will break down. Moreover, break down within the human biological system manifests itself largely as cardiovascular disturbances, e.g. high blood pressure, heart disease, diabetes, etc. It may even manifest itself as psychological imbalances, e.g. depression, loner behavior, bipolarism, etc. all of which pose long-term danger to the one experiencing them.

As in the example of confronting the bully, as well as the natural design of the human system to deal with stress, the painful events of our past exhibited control over us through fear, and the delicateness of our younger years prevented a fight response. Therefore, we succumb to the fear, and our systems chose flight (repression) instead.

Now that we have provided some understanding of why we responded the way we did; we should now understand that it wasn't our fault. We are not responsible for the harm done to us! We didn't do anything wrong! We were not equipped to deal with such traumatic events at such a young age! It's not our fault! Our parents, if present while the event occurred, perhaps would have helped us! After all, it is the responsibility of the parents to provide love and protection to their kids, until which time they are able to handle these events on their own. But something went wrong, and now not only are we impacted, but our parents are, as well as the perpetrators of the injustice. We now are all in need of healing, and part of the solution is to be reconciled to the pain of our past.

In order to be reconciled to our past, we must realize that we are a product of our past. We are, in essence, the sum total of our life experiences. Our past, no matter how painful it may be, has served to shape who we are. Those experiences have either made us stronger or weaker, better or worse, stable or unstable. We are a living past, stamping out and moving towards our future. To deny your past would be to deny a part of you. That event, which we hate to remember, is as much a part of you as the happiest time that you can bring to remembrance! Let's travel back in time to one of my past experiences.

I grew up in a typical large southern family. There were fifteen of which six were boys and nine were girls. We were all close in age, in most cases separated by a little more than a gestation period. My father and mother were together, though my mother had two children from a previous marriage and my father had children from many relationships, at the time unbeknownst to us. My father was a good provider. He worked diligently to ensure that we had food to eat and clothes to wear. My mother was a good nurturer and housewife, who, on occasion, worked for many white families as a housekeeper. Because of their efforts, I grew up unaware that we were poor and barely making, as they say in the South, "ends meat". On the surface, we were the typical African-American family trying to forge a living in a newly political-initiated, but cultural unaccepted integrated South. My father experienced much hardship trying to provide for his functional family, and incurred even much more stress because of the social pressures of the time. I found that he would drink and womanize as a means of coping and dealing with the pressures of his time. He spent very little time at home. He rarely interacted with my mother. She loved him; I could see it in her eyes. I believe, in some twisted and unhealthy way, he loved her as well. However, the way he expressed his love was unhealthy. My father would scream and become angry with my mother and with us for no apparent reason. He would throw things, hurl expletives, and withdraw from my mother. The emotional toll on her must have been unbearable. However, she always kept her silence.

As kids, we couldn't do much. We heard the arguments, saw the callousness my father showed towards our mother, but because of our age, we remained silent. We grew up watching these feats of anger and lack of demonstration of love towards the family. The only time we would see our family demonstrate love is with the aid of alcohol. He would drink and then tell us he loved us! In some strange way, we were glad to hear it for deep down in our souls we also wanted to feel it from him. We received it, but his drinking tarnished it. My mother received the same message, but she would push him away and tell him that she was aware of the outside secretive life that he was living. Nevertheless, she stayed with him. After all, where would an African-American woman with a six-grade education and fifteen kids go! Therefore, the family stayed intact, but we were subjected to the pain of a dysfunctional family. Our souls were scarred! We looked, listened, learned and we kept it all in. With the concealment came resentment, dissociative behavior, and a catalyst towards repeating behavior that would continue to hurt those we professed to love.

I grew up and pushed with extraordinary determination to achieve what the circumstances of my parent's time prohibited them from achieving—a high school diploma. My mother, unfortunately, only had a sixth-grade education, and my father a ninth-grade education. They were exceptionally smart individuals, but the circumstances of the times did not afford them to continue their education. I graduated high school, attended college, and went to graduate school (not bad for a poor Mississippi boy growing up in the racially torn South). I not only obtained my high school diploma, but in the end, I was to have four colleges degrees. My achievements were all fueled by my unwillingness to duplicate my childhood family experiences. I figured if I obtained what my parents didn't obtain—education, wealth, etc. I'd be a better person. I wouldn't be like my father, but I was wrong. I was the sum total of my past experiences. Deep down inside, I still remembered the painful childhood I had! I remembered the sorrow and hurt on my mother's face, brought about by the traumatic experiences she endured for the sake of her kids. Moreover, I would weep. My soul was scarred! No matter how hard I tried, I still was, inside, that person that I dreaded being!

The question was, how was I to become a better person? —for I needed to be a better person for myself and for those that were in relationship with me. My soul needed healing! I kept the pain inside for so long, hiding it but all the while using it as fuel to propel myself forward. It was killing me! And eventually, what was inside would begin to show itself to those I loved.

After I got married, at some point I began demonstrating similar behavior to that of my father! I was not as bad but bad enough to affect the emotional well-being of those who loved me. At some point, I realized that what I was seeing on the outside was a good indication of what was going on in the inside. My soul, my emotional health had deteriorated to a point where it began affecting others. Out of love for my wife, my family, and myself, I realized that I had to get a grip. I realized that I had to seek to restore harmony within my life. And in order to accomplish that, I knew I had to face the demons of my past. I knew I had to overcome them, accept what they had done in my life, no matter how painful, and begin to move towards being a better husband, a better father, a better me.

As I looked back at my past, I realized that I was repeating what my father had demonstrated during my childhood. I accepted the damage as something devastating, but now no longer having the power to impact my life, and I resolved to use it to effectuate positive change within my life. I knew it was not going to be easy but I knew it had to happen. If there was any hope of breaking the chains of my past and moving on to my future, I had to be reconciled to my past.

To be reconciled to the pain of our past merely means to face it as unpleasant as it was. We must face it if we are to ever move on; if we are ever achieved wholeness and true happiness. Our emotional state, and perhaps our physical state, is beginning to show signs of a system that has been imbalanced for years. Our soul is unhappy, and as a result, it is beginning to show itself. We must work to bring about harmony to our emotional state so that we might live happy, prosperous, healthy, and whole lives. We must find a way to be reconciled to the very thing that has been working to destroy us over the years. We must overcome the fear and devastation of the past, and in order to do this, reconciliation must take place. If you can't find a way to do this within yourself, remember you do not have to go it alone. There are a number of groups, psychologist, psycho-therapists, counselors all trained, willing, and waiting to assist you in confronting the pains of your past. All you need to do, is take the first step in deciding you need to do this, and then give one of them a call! It is essential!

Here's a bit of additional advice. You've heard that love covers a multitude of sin. Well, love is a powerful overcomer of pain, trauma, and resistance to change; no matter how deep the pain! No matter how much that person or persons hurt you! You must find love within yourself. You must find that God-given love that is a grace to overcome! Perfect love drives out all fear! If you find yourself yielding again to the stifling pains of past events, look for love within to overcome the situation. Perhaps it may help to consider that the individual that hurt you is God's creation as well. Perhaps it might help to consider that the person that hurt you is someone's child. Perhaps it might help to consider that by chance, their childhood may have been filled with atrocity, and as a result, they are merely repeating the hurt and pain that they experienced at a young age. I know it doesn't seem fair, but it will help you bring out the love for humanity that we all have within.

There is a concept within the field of counseling that is termed, "wounded healer". The concept applies to any individual who has experience some hurt or pain and has learned to find healing through helping others. Within this concept lies an underlying love for humanity. Within this concept, a sacred wisdom reveals that healing comes through helping others. Healing comes through expressing and sharing a reconciled event with others, so that they can begin the road towards healing, and so that you can move down the road of healing as well.

The bible says that Jesus was "wounded for our transgressions, bruised for our iniquities, the chastisement of our peace was upon him and by His stripes, we were healed". This historical text is a living and breathing organism for those who choose to believe. This is the greatest example of the concept of wounded healer that one can ever search out. One Divine Man, working through the power of the Holy Ghost, to yield one ultimate sacrifice, so that others may be healed and reconciled into eternal life. This is the greatest exploit ever historically or futuristically, that can ever be done to heal the broken hearted and wounded souls.

We, like Christ, must be willing to act in love in order to embrace the unpleasant pains of our past and overcome them! In so doing, we not only recognize that the events of the past shape who we are today, but the experience itself can serve as an impetus that will drive us and those associated with us towards achieving wholeness. It will be a principle by which, if employed continually to daily life, change can result and happiness can be obtained.

Can you imagine if we all reconciled to the pain of our past? What would the world be like? What would our kids look like? I have to believe it will be a better place, for all of the brokenness that plagues so many would be under control. The pains of our past will no longer be concealed causing emotional, physical, and psychological damage to us. No longer will the repressed events of our past be acted out on those that we love. Did you know that if you want to see the harmful effects of adults, who have lived through traumatic childhoods and subsequently become fathers, have on society? All you have to do is look at current census data. If you did, you would see these alarming facts: Fatherless homes account for 63% of youth suicides, 90% are homeless/runaway children, 85% of children have behavior problems, 71% are high school dropouts, 85% of youths are in prison, and well over 50% are teen mothers. More recently, the teenage pregnancy rate has risen, and is currently at a rate higher than it has been over the last ten years.

I believe that at the root cause of these alarming statistics is an adult who never dealt with his childhood, and as a result, never matured to the point where they could be a loving, nurturing, caring, providing, protecting, and emotionally present father, one who makes a visible difference in the lives of his children. The fathers have to be present and active in the lives of the children, in order to change these statistics! The fathers not only have to be present, but they have to be whole. They must be reconciled to the pain of their past, in order to position themselves to stop the vicious cycle that leads to the downfall of their youth, and to the downfall of society as a whole.

Not only do we see the effects of wounded fathers through the statistics of our youth, but we can see the impact through the number of men in prison today, especially the number of African-American men. African American men make up twenty-five percent of those that commit crimes, and seventy-five percent of them are convicted and are subsequently imprisoned, while African American's represent only twelve percent of the United States population! There is something desperately wrong with these figures at large and the incarceration figures in particular! I understand that the system is not favorable towards minorities. But I also understand as well that not everyone imprisoned is innocent. Most have acted out behavior that caused them to end up in prison.

I have heard of the stories from countless men who say that they felt they had no choice but to behave in a criminal manner. I have heard the stories of the men who say that their fathers were criminals, or they didn't know their father's, as their fathers died when they were toddlers either because they were murdered, contracted AIDS or their father's whereabouts were unknown to them or their mothers. These stories all reek of devastation. They reek of a painful past that have gone unreconciled, and the time has come that we begin the road to healing. We must embrace change if we are to ever fulfill our God-given destiny upon the earth. The entire world is waiting for the hurt, bruised, battered, and disenfranchised to embrace change, recall, reconcile their past in order for love to abide.

The politico-judicial-educational system in America is no friend of the African American male. As I mentioned earlier,

African American men make up the majority of those convicted of crimes and those imprisoned. Additionally, almost 20% of African American men between the ages of 16 to 29 years of age are unemployed, compared to 7.9% of white men of the same age group. 10.1% of African American men between the ages of 18 to 29 years of age are in prison, compared to 1.5% of white men of the same age group. Only 7.5% of African American men between the ages of 18 to 29 graduate from college, compared to 17.3% of their white counterparts of the same age group. (Census Bureau; Current Population Survey Table, accessed online, July 2006) The system has done an atrocious job on the African American male.

I view these figures as indicators of the emotional state of African Americans in general, and African American males in particular. At work within a system that functions to exclude, undermine and eliminate the African American contribution to society, is an undercurrent of emotional instability. How can one be emotionally healthy, when decade in and decade out, generation in and generation out, they see so many talented and gifted men being eaten up in the system? It is not that these men choose to be eaten up but the system is designed to eat them up, and only through an awareness of the system and careful navigation through it, can one hope to escape it.

Bottled up within the souls of the African American male is anger and frustration! They are angry because the system is unfair! They are angry because the system is against them, and does not give them equal opportunity to succeed! They are frustrated because, they play by the rules, but the rules were subject to change unannounced, and all the while, the game is still being played! This is what the African American male is exposed to constantly! Politicians try to trivialize it, but the fact that this is what African American males are experiencing shows up in bureau statistics. Many African American males are killing one another! Black on black crime is on the rise! Suicides among African Americans are on the rise, all the while, the image of African Americans is continuing to erode.

Turn on the television, and the image of the African American male you see is one that is unintelligent and not well spoken. Flip to another channel, and the image portrayed of the African American male is one who is a drug dealer, or one that is portraying him as a violent criminal! Try to escape the media by going to the movies, and you see more of the same! African Americans are bombarded by negative images, and those images are working as part of a larger system to destabilize, dehumanize and denigrate people of African American descent. The result to date is a people who are in need of emotional healing; perhaps total healing.

I believe that a vital part of the process to acquiring healing is releasing. We must release ourselves from the grips of the oppressive system that is bent on keeping us down and tiring us out. The release has to be done emotionally first, and then as we continue to work towards achieving real equality in this society, we will break from the system that works tirelessly to trap us.

Releasing means refusing to allow the system to get you down. It means never telling yourself "no", when the system is trying to get you to give up! You must always keep in mind that you are a part of a greater cause, a greater movement! I talked earlier in this book about how the African American heritage is one that places the male at the center of his family, and as a major positive contributor to his community. We must not forget this, as we encounter opposition to our struggle to be restored to our rightful place within society. We must be determined and disciplined, working to achieve greater, not just for ourselves, but for the greater community. We must not forget the sacrificial spirit of those who came before us.

In order for greater achievement, we must not be hindered by the pains and misfortunes of our past. We must use them as a catalyst for change. We must remember and be reconciled to the pain of our past, but we must release the pain to God for He alone is able to handle our weight and burdens that we may be currently experiencing and the weight and burdens of those that came before us. There is healing in releasing the pain of your past. One cannot run forward speedily nor efficiently or effectively if he/she is carrying additional weight. The weight must be shed in order for them to proceed in a manner that maximizes their strengths and showcases their talents.

While suffering and dying on the cross, Jesus said of his persecutors, "Father, forgive them, for they know not what they do" (Luke 23:34, KJV) In this text, Jesus is suffering and laying down His life for something that He did not do. His life was a propitiation for our sins. Yet, in its climatic moment of sacrifice, Jesus cries out to His father in heaven and asks for forgiveness for those who are carrying out the dreadful deed! Jesus releases the acts of the people exercised on Him and towards Him, and proceeds to continue along His destiny.

I believe that the message being sent and the lesson being taught by Jesus during this great moment of sacrifice is the principle of releasing. We must release individuals from the acts that they have exercised towards us, no matter how devastating. Slavery was a travesty! Racism and discrimination are unjust! Systematic oppression is burdening, but we must release it all unto our Father in heaven, if we are to continue on along the destiny that God has for us! God has hopes and plans for us and we are expected to achieve them. We must not allow anything to keep us from achieving our destiny! We, therefore, must release anything that can hinder us, so that we might run on freely and with liberty.

Releasing has therapeutic benefits. We must release individual(s) from the acts that they have exercised towards us, not for them, but for ourselves. If we do not release them; we give them power over us. The acts that they exercised towards us will continue to plague us, slowly weighing us down until we come to a halt. We must release the burdens for ourselves and not just for them. We cannot give control to anyone and anything other than almighty God. Jesus is Lord and Him only, and if we work under His lordship, we are free to move forward and bring about change in our lives and the lives of our families and communities. Change is facilitated by releasing the burdens of your past and forgiving those who have hurt you. Releasing will free you to run forward and accomplish the things that God has created you to accomplish. It is important to release for ourselves, as well as forgiving those who hurt us.

We need to be whole again! We need to heal the fragmentation that has so easily denied us of peace, joy and happiness! Achieving wholeness will allow is to be free! Whom the Lord sets free is free indeed! Then and only then can we say that we decide to wear the mask, the mask does not wear us!

CHAPTER 12

"Free Your Mind"

»———————«

Everything that I have written thus far has been to increase your awareness and educate you on your true history versus the story you have been deceived to believe is yours! It has been written to begin to move you towards healing and wholeness! Central to healing and wholeness is the need to free your mind! Freeing our minds of clutter! Eliminating that which stresses us and keeps us all pinned up will ultimately hurt us! Real change comes about through tension! The application of tension to that which we see as the norm is a requirement for change.

Docility only contributes to the perpetuating the status quo. In fact, docility is what the old slave master forced upon Africans who were enslaved! If I can get you to be dependent on the system then it is the system that controls you and not you yourself. Docility strips you of your individuality, your liberty and your self-worth! Docility is the weapon of the enemy by which your talents, gifts, strengths are manipulated and used for the enemy's good and leaves you to live or survive on the scraps that the enemy provides and he only gives you that to keep you alive so that he can rape you of your talent again.

For far too long have we used our gifts and our talents to make everyone else rich. For far too long we have minimized our aspirations and hopes in order to fit into a society that was never designed to help propel us to greater success! The intent of the original Founders Fathers was to establish a community where Europeans who were relegated to the bottom of the European social structure, could make their own way of the social ladder and establish wealth for themselves. They did this without care or concern for the life of anyone that didn't look like them. This is evident from their raping Native Americans of their land and killing anyone who got in their way. They might have justified it as the spoils of war but there wasn't a war initially. What happened was an intentional diabolical plan to take by any means necessary. Once they had the land and had reduced the Native American population through war and hard labor, they then had to think of another way to build their society so they then put in place a plan to rob and exploit Africans of their skill, talent, and abilities. This is the foundation of this country and it was never intended to be an inclusive society but an exclusive one. But now that we are here and have lend our talents and abilities to build this nation, we are entitled to take part in it on equal footing so we need our minds free to bring about equity for our people. It's time now to leave the burdens of our past behind and began to free ourselves so that we might work without hinderance to bring to fruition a nation with expanded ideals. Ideals that include all men, regardless of race, creed or color. Ideals that present equal opportunity for all of humankind. It's like that lyrical prophet Jay Z says: Gone brush your shoulders off! I dare you to gone brush your shoulders off and pursue greatness! Gone brush your shoulders off and purpose your dreams! Make your dreams a reality! Change your outlook and move to your next!

If you truly want change; if you truly want to be free you must be willing to challenge your current beliefs and risk moving out of your comfort zone. We must conduct self-inventory of who we are as an individual and once this is done be willing to rid ourselves of what does not propel us to freedom! I am who I think I am! I will be what I allow myself to be exposed to! I am the sum total of my environment. If your environment is hindering you, change your environment. If your relationships are hindering you, forge new relationships! If your past pain is impacting how you engage positively in the world, seek counseling! We must free ourselves of the impediments to success; the hurdles of life that causes us to waste value time of which we are limited!

Also, of special note, is that we have to refuse to be distracted! We must understand that the enemy uses misdirection as weapon to get us off of our purpose. It is one of his greatest weapons! It is almost like when you are focused on executing a plan for a project that you have already thought through. You understand what needs to happen. You have worked through the potential pitfalls that might slow up your progress. You understand the rewards and benefits of the project. It looks like everything is an all clear but then a shiny object appears out of nowhere! The shiny object is strongly drawing your attention! It looks good! It sounds good! It smells good! It gives the impression that it is a better project than the one you spent so long planning! As a result, you shift all of your focus to the shiny object! In the end, you find out that the shiny object was just that a shiny object, devoid of substance and real merit! You wasted so much time going after the shiny object that it made it impossible to deliver on the project that you had already thoroughly planned. Now, you have no reward to show for it! This is the plan of the enemy. He uses misdirection to keep you from achieving your goals! We must not get distracted! We must not lose focus! We have to be aware of the wiles of the enemy and beat him at his game! In so doing, you will free your mind of distraction so that you might be able to live freely.

An integral part to freeing our minds also includes demonstrating emotional intelligence. We must possess the ability, the capacity to be aware of, control and express emotions in a healthy and productive manner. It is a sign of maturity, yes, but more importantly it demonstrates your ability to work as an integral part of a team. It is an important part of functioning with family and within society.

We are always depicted as being angry, hot tempered and ready to fly off at the drop of a dime! This is not our natural propensity but it is the perception forced upon us! We must train ourselves to remain calm, cool and collected so that have an opportunity to present our thoughts clearly, strategically and effectively. It is important for us to be on the playing field; to get into the game and not be excluded from it! Once we are in the game we are seated at the table! Being seated at the table allows us to begin to subtly release our plan to effectual change! Then we will be able to build the ladder of success so that others will have that path to follow.

We have got rid of the baggage that the enemy used to degrade us mentally! You know with words like you can't handle complexity! It's too hard for you grasp or understand! These are the tricks that the enemy plays on us to lower our self-esteem! Don't' fall for it! Cleanse your mind of them! I know they may have assigned you to Special Ed at a young age and that crippled you psychologically. It was devastating but you got through it! That was then but this is now! You control your destiny! You are not dumb! You are good enough! You are intelligent and you process unique skill and talents! Everything that you need is inside of you! Let go of the baggage and move freely!

Then we have to overturn the brain washing that generation after generation has wreaked on us! Brainwashing and propaganda designed to condition and make you believe that white is better! There ice is not colder! There goods are not better! They can't always do it better! They don't always have the answer! All of this is designed to make you hate yourself; to make you hate blackness! White people are not better than you! Poor white people are not better than you! In fact, no of us are better than each other! And no blacks are not the only ones killing blacks! I've dealt with this earlier in the book! Yes, blacks kill blacks but white kill whites too! Worse even worse is that whites are killing whites but they are killing blacks at a dipropionate high number. They are doing the most killing not you! They are just trying to perpetuate black hate! You are not a killer! You give life! You are excellent just the way you are! God made you that way and nobody can ever be a better you than you!

What do we do to make our lives consistently better after we cleared our minds in search of freedom? We have to begin to involve ourselves in healthy counseling! That's a must! We must gravitate to things that are positive; that are of a good report! We have to stop using negative words! Find positive words to use! Make an intentional effort to show love and kindness! Hang around good people! Exercise! Take care of your body! Eat the right foods! Got the doctor to get annual checkups! Insist on getting prostate exams, colonoscopy and high blood pressure checks! Ask for forgiveness from anyone you have wronged! Forgive those who have wronged you! All of this will help you to live a healthy, positive and clean life! It will help you to reduce stress and breathe deeply the liberating air of freedom!

CHAPTER 13

Breathe Freely

Admittedly, the air of which we breathe has been toxic for so long! Racism has polluted the air of this country for generations making it utterly difficult for anyone of color to breathe easily! It is time, however, for us to change the air we breathe! Filter out the toxicities that seek to cutoff and strangle our breathing! The filter that we are to apply is the removal of the blindfold off of those that stand by on the sidelines watching injustice occur. We must take the blindfold off of those who say they are not racist but refuse to step in and use their systematically afforded privilege to help dismantle racism. If not, then unfortunately they are correctly labeled a racist and are the problem and not considered innocent. For too long America has had its knee on the neck of black men and women remanding us to the margins of society leaving very little space to breathe!

The time is up for standing on the sidelines! We must all get in the game! Time out for relegating blacks to the margins of entertainment where we exist just for their pleasure! Time Out for black on black crime where we are killing off our future! Time out for self-deprecation and living beneath our God-given privilege of human decency! By doing so we cleanse the air we breathe!

While its time out for toxicities of racism, oppression, marginalization and dehumanization, it's time in for self-empowerment, self-respect, self-elevation, self-authentication! We must walk in these elements and more so that we begin to cleanse the air of toxicity and breathe deeply the cleanse air of righteousness, justice, love, kindness, care and concern for all humankind!

With our great history! With a move towards wholeness and healing! With us taking the necessary steps to free our minds and live fully authenticated! We can cleanse the air we breathe! We can help to remove the blindfolds of those who belong to the group that oppress us in hope of us coming together to remove this toxicity from the country in which we all live! We can begin to breathe freely! We can permanently remove the mask we wear and move within society in the way God intended us too! You are somebody! You have purpose! You belong here! You are valuable! The entire world needs you to survive and thrive! You the descendant of original man and without you there is no other!

We must take a deep breath! Inhale and exhale purposely with the realization that God gave us life and not man and no man can take away from you want God has given you! Take a deep breath then take a broad step forward! Dream big! Aim high! Don't effort doubt yourself! Stop thinking you are too small! Stop thinking you don't have what it takes! Stop thinking you are not good enough! Never tell yourself no! Give it your all! Start all over if you have to! Breathe deeply and exhale! You've have been holding your breath way too long! Stoke the courage lost! Fan the fire of hope and achievement! Build your confidence to live in society with the same intensity and focus that you bring to the game you love! Whether it's chess, basketball, pool, tennis, football, golf. Whatever your passion, begin to approach life with that same level of purpose; that same level of focus; that same level of confidence; that same level of pride and courage! I challenge you to find your purpose! Walk in your purpose! There is more in you than you think! The earth is your canvas paint whatever you like! No man can hinder you! Take a deep breath and breathe freely! You are on your way up!

Once we begin to breathe freely and approach life with courage and boldness, fearlessness and purpose, we will move into the phase of life where we live in our privilege!

The whites in America move about with ease; without a care in the world, why? Because of their privilege! We have to create our own sphere of privilege and move therein! We can go into a restaurant and if we are not welcome there; use your privilege to not spend your money there! If you are denied your rights on any occasion, use your privilege to demand justice; don't just let it go but pursue what is right! If they do it to you, they will do it to others! Use your privilege to correct wrong and bring about justice! If they try to exclude you from business! Start your own business and if you fail, keep trying again and again and again! You will be successful! Take a deep breathe a try it again! Breathe freely! Move freely! You belong here!

CHAPTER 14

Mask Off

All of what I've written thus far was to help us achieve this! To revitalize our communities! To restore our families! To live freely, justly and without shame! To restore the natural order of things, were we are contributing to the elevation of society and the world. Where we are no longer depicted as the least of these but are acknowledge as the gem of society; the enablers of freedom and justice! The givers of life! No longer having to hide behind a mask or minimize our self-worth! But live like a man! Strong, sensitive, loving, caring, resourceful, innovator, intelligent, responsible family men who are of good character bearing a good name!

As I have previously delineated, slavery, as well as the current governmental system of today, has done an atrocious job on the African American Male. He has been excluded from positive contribution to society, as well as from positively contributing to his family and community. This has been the case for generations. Not only will raising the economic and social level of the African American male be enough to restore our families and communities, but there is a need for work to be done on his psyche.

Sadly, sixty percent of African American families are fatherless and for the remaining forty percent that are not, many of the fathers are present in body only, and are not actively engaged in the rearing of their children or the affirmation and nurturing of their spouse. Edwin Louis Cole makes the following statement regarding the fathers of today: "Today, instead of the absentee father being the curse of our day, it is 'fatherlessness.' The difference is that rather than being absent from the family, there is an absence of concern for the family. Fatherlessness is the curse of our day."

We must work to change the psyche of the African American male, in a way that regains the attitudes that his forefathers demonstrated towards their children and family. Programs must be put in place that re-teach the African American male what his role is within his family, and how to carry out that role. The African American male has to be re-taught what it means to be a man, a father, and to be a husband. The African American male must be taught in hopes of gaining an understanding the impact of his presence, position and paternal values. This must be done in order for our families to achieve wholeness, as well as restore a positive image and vitality of the male within his family and community.

The programs needed to transform the attitudes of the African American male are critical to the success of our communities. The African American male must be taught the history of his role within the family and community. He must be taught in a manner that underscores the need for him to regain his rightful place within his family and community, for in so doing, it will be therapeutic for him as well as for his community. Edwin H. Friedman puts it this way: "…not only does our position in our extended families affect how we function in other relationships, but also the efforts to gain better differentiation of self in that extended field will have corresponding effects at home, at work, and on our health. The more we can understand our own origins, the more we can sympathize with theirs; the more we can define our own families, the more we can help them modify the influence of, or mobilize the strengths in, theirs. And the more we realize how difficult it can be to gain any measure of self-differentiation, the more humbly we can appreciate their plight."

Edwin H. Friedman delineates the need to understand our origins. He underscores the interrelatedness of an individual and his family and community; how they need each other to survive. It is the lack of this interrelatedness within the African American communities that have caused them to deteriorate, and the people to lack focus and drive. Restoration of the transformed, mentally and socially adjusted African American male to his role within family and community, will initiate a revolution within it and will serve to promote emotional health and decrease fragmentation.

As you can see, real change is need for, in the words of Margaret Kornfeld when speaking on first order change (personal change) versus second order change (change that effects a group): "When people make a first order change, they do so within their present system or circumstance. With a second order change, they change the system, or circumstance itself." (Margaret Kornfeld) In first order change people, adjust to their present situation. They learn to function better but their present situation does not change. A second order change is a paradigmatic shift in which a whole constellation of beliefs, attitudes, and actions are altered because of a new perception of reality. In second order change, a whole system is changed. African Americans in general and African American men in particular are in need of second order change. We must be transformed in a way that not only benefits ourselves, but in a way that benefits society.

It is critical that the approach used to restore the African American male to his family and community be done in a manner that celebrates his value and does not ostracize him for past failures. We must seek to restore him in a manner that is reflective of our love and deep concern for his well-being, and demonstrate that we are ecstatic because of his return. We must be careful not to attack or appear defensive of our homes. We must be open and willing to dedicate ourselves to a journey that will be mutually beneficial, no matter how rough the journey may be in the beginning.

In addition to our being open and receptive of the African American male's return to his family, it will be even more important for the African American male to be open and remain open to the change that is occurring in his life. He must be open to returning home and to his community again. It is critical that he sees his value within the family and within his community. He must understand that he has something to contribute to the well-being of the family and community, and therefore, present himself with the confidence that he will make a difference. An embracing of who he is and what he has to offer, as well as an understanding of the dynamics of the family and community and how he can contribute, will be most important to his restoration. Monica McGoldrick, renowned family therapist, states regarding the family wholeness: "The fundamental guideline for going home again is: Don't attack and don't defend. Going home again means finding a way to be yourself and stay connected to your family without defending yourself or attacking others. The typical dysfunctional roles people get into in their families—in which one becomes the caretaker and the other the caretaker or one always pursues and the other distances—develop because family members have not evolved sufficient sense of self to function for themselves."

As we have delineated earlier, the root cause of destructive behavior exhibited by the African American male lies within family function. Moreover, it is steeped in his world-view perception and definition of family. His family is not only his immediate family, but encompasses his entire community, and is shaped by a need to contribute to community. Restoration, therefore, must begin here with the family. However, at the very center of the African American culture is the church. Traditionally, the African American is very spiritual. Their hope is to live a life that is pleasing and mindful of a higher calling. The church is a family member to the African American. God is the head of the family and the community. God is their source, and without Him they cannot do anything. It is therefore most important that the church have a direct role in restoring the African American male to his central role within the family and community. The church must be actively engaged in the process. The messages delivered by the church must be relevant, empowering and liberating. They must be authentic and reflective of a prophetic word that restores, regenerates, and rebuilds the soul, character, and mind of the African American male.

The church must be willing, ready and able to take direct action from a social justice perspective, in order to right the wrongs of injustice that plague the African American community in particular and minorities at large. The church must be involved in social justice, else the preaching, teaching, shouting and praising will be less than authentic. They must be directly involved in letting their voice be heard within the halls of justice without fear of retaliation. The church must represent and take on a sacrificial role just as Christ did, if the hopes of a new community will ever be realized.

J. Philip Wogaman articulated this most succinctly when he said "Christian thought devoid of action is inauthentic;" and Martin Luther King in his letter from the Birmingham jail, articulated the need for the church to be engaged in direct action without fear of retaliation when he said: "We who engage in nonviolent direct action are not the creators of tension. We merely bring to the surface the hidden tension that is already alive." Martin understood that the church holds a powerful position within the African American community, and its involvement must be solicited if true change is to be realized within it. The church must be willing, ready, able and authentic in its involvement in revitalizing, healing and restoration of the African American male to his family and community.

Once we as a people work together purposely to achieve all of this and then some, will we be fully restored to our rightful place! We will be positioned to walk in our privilege and release lovingly the peace of God that passeth all understanding to all of humankind for we are the original torchbearers and without us the land cannot prosper; the people cannot prosper and life can never be free!

Sermonette 1

»» ———————— ««

Exodus 14:13–19;25

I'd like to start off this sermon with a declaration! A declaration that lays the foundation for a reason to celebrate! A declaration that was scripted by the sacrificial pen of one locked behind the bars of the Birmingham jail!

"Abused and scorned though we may be, our destiny is tied up with America's destiny. Before the Pilgrims landed at Plymouth, we were here. Before the pen of Jefferson etched the majestic words of the Declaration of Independence across the pages of history, we were here." (Martin Luther King, Jr.)

That's right we were here long before the Nina, the Pinta and the Santa Maria hit the shores of the Islands of Hispaniola! We were here long before the Portuguese slave ship called the San Juan Batista was enroute to Mexico (Veracruz) from Angola West Africa with some 350 captives crammed within its bowels, was raided and some 20 Africans taken and traded as goods in what history records as Jamestown, Virginia!

History records that long before slavery our Ancestors traded as far East as Europe and Asian and as far West as North America using the Windward Trade winds off the coast of Africa and the ocean currents! We are not are new people! We are an ancient people! Responsible for agriculture, architecture, religion, math and philosophy! We are an Ancient people! Our pasts are filled with mighty exploits! So much so that the rest of the world envied and sought to steal from us, kill us and destroy our way of living! Hence, worldwide slavery of African ensued!

In the words of MLK, I'm here to tell you that the struggle to reclaim our past still ensues! In the words of MLK I declare to you today that:

"The Emancipation Proclamation of 1863 did not bring full freedom to the Negro, for although he enjoyed certain political and social opportunities during Reconstruction, the Negro soon discovered that the pharaohs of the South were determined to keep him in slavery"

I take up a rather familiar story, where the children of Israel had been enslaved for some 430 years! The people had cried unto the Lord and He heard their cry and now has reared up Moses to emancipate the people of God from their bondage!

We take up at the text a little later in the journey after the Lord spake unto Moses saying: when Pharaoh had let the people go, don't take the short route because the short route thou it may seem quick and easy it is the way of the Philistines for they would wage war and in the eyes of the people after 430 years of hardship if the people had to fight wars for their freedom they might lose hope and decide that it wasn't worth it and turn back! So, God led the people about, through the way of the wilderness of the Red Sea. And they took their journey and encamped at the edge of the wilderness and the Lord went before them in a cloud by day leading the way and in a pillar of fire by night to give them light. But while they were moving in their new found freedom, pharaoh up and changes his mind and decides to go after the people of God to enslave them once again! Let me side bar here! That's what is going on in America today! The spirits of the pharaohs of old are working in the pharaohs of today still determined to keep God's people in slavery!

We have endured slavery! We have come through Jim Crow! We have built this country through our knowledge, skill, craftmanship and labor! Established the riches thereof through forced servitude in the rice patties of South Carolina; the tobacco fields of North Carolina, the sugar plantations of Louisiana, even the cotton fields of Mississippi! We are responsible for creating the very fabric of American society stitch by stitch and we refuse to go back!

I say boldly saying Pharaoh wants us back but those days are over! Refuse to go back but that's not all! I boldly declare that we want what's ours! We don't' want it all but we want what's ours! Forty acres and a mule were promised but delivered! Separate but equal was a position of pacifism but it wasn't sufficient! Affirmative Action was noble attempt at equality but it was a failed attempt! We demand not just equality! We demand equity!

We demand what is rightfully ours! We demand attain the full citizenship that this nation's constitution affords us! We demand to be free from systematic oppression! Free from covert and overt racism! Free from dehumanization and wrongful criminalization! We are the representatives of the blood, sweat and tears of our ancestors and we declare not only we will not go back but we want what's ours!

Like today, the country's leadership appears to have hardened its heart and tries to take us back just like pharaoh of old! But God! But God has a plan and a purpose! He has a plan and a purpose for us and he has a plan and a purpose for pharaoh!

Now let me get back to this sermon! You see, the story is a story that stretches back thousands of years! Our people had been enslaved for some 430 years! The people had cried unto the Lord and He heard their cry and now He has reared up Moses to free His people!

We take up at the text a little later in the journey after the Lord spoke unto Moses saying: when Pharaoh had let the people go, don't take the short route because the short route thou it may seem quick and easy but it is the way of the Philistines for they would wage war and in the eyes of the people after so much hardship the people won't be able to muster up enough strength to fight for their freedom! They might lose hope and decide that it's not worth it and turn back!

So, God led the people about, through the way of the wilderness of the Red Sea. And they took their journey and encamped at the edge of the wilderness and the Lord went before them by day in a cloud leading the way and by night in a pillar of fire to give them light. But while they are moving in their new found freedom, pharaoh changes his mind and decides to go after the people of God to enslave them once again! The people of God in their journey towards freedom now appears as though they are stuck between a rock and a hard place! They have the Red Sea before them and they have the enemy coming behind them! That's where we take up this text! When the pharaoh drew nigh, the children of Israel lifted up their eyes, and the Egyptians marched after them and they were sore afraid and they cried out unto the Lord. And they said unto Moses, because there were no graves in Egypt, hast thou taken us away to die in the wilderness!

What do you do when it looks like the same God that you counted on to deliver you appears to have abandoned you? What do you do when it feels as though the one you counted on is nowhere to be found? I'm glad you asked! We've got to realize that the same God that had the power to deliver you then is the same God that has the power to keep you now! The same God that had the power to deliver us, is the same God that has the power to keep us! The same God that had the power to deliver us the first time, is the same God that has the power to keep us! When we run up against hard places, our declaration cannot be that of the Israelites, we must stand flat footed and declare I still believe! I believe He's a Deliverer! I believe He's a Keeper! I believe He's a Way maker! I believe and I'm standing! Come what may, I will still stand! I will stand with my loins gird about with truth! I will stand holding the shield of Faith! I will stand and when I've done all to stand! I will keep on standing! Because I believe God! And I'm standing on the promises of God!

I heard the words of the hymnists: He didn't bring me this far to leave me! And He didn't bring you this far to leave you! There will be mountains I'll have to climb; battles I'll have to fight I just can't give up now! I've come to far from where I started from! Nobody told me the road would be easy! I don't believe He's brought me this far to leave me!

Verse 13 says Moses said unto the people, Fear ye not, stand still, and see the salvation of the Lord! And that's the Lord's declaration to us today! Fear not, hold your peace and see with your own eyes the salvation of the Lord! Fear not hold your peace!

Recognize what's going on around you and don't be a bystander! Get active in the Game! Our time is coming! Indeed, our time is now! Activate your Faith! Make things happen! Use the power you have within your sphere of influence! Begin to establish your tomorrow! The Lord is with you! He holds you in His right hand and He will not suffer you to be moved!

They grumbled at Moses and Moses tried to calm the people but inside he's crying out to God and the Lord responds: Lift up thou ROD! It is significant that he says lift up thou Rod! His Rod and not a spear! His Rod and not a shield! His Rod and not a stone! He says lift up thou Rod! The Rod has had various meanings and uses in the ancient times! At times it was used as a support to help one who is feeble to walk but that's not what the Lord is referring to! There is a Rod that Sheepherders would use to herd the sheep but that's not what the Lord is referring to either! What the reader has to understand is that the Rod being used in this context is of a prophetic purpose! You see when you study the Word of God, you'll see in Hebrew's chapter 9 speaks of Aaron's rod! Aaron's rod was a budding rod and was a symbol of Christ eternal reign! If you flip over to Michal chapter 5 and verse 1 you see that the minor prophet prophesies that the coming of our Lord and our savior will be preceded by the carrying of the rod! And if you visit the Psalms volume 2 and verse 9 the Psalmist declares that Jesus, I said Jesus achieves victory with a rod! So, when Moses lift's up the rod before the enemy that is approaching! In one fell swoop Moses is declaring the sovereignty, the authority of the Lord Jesus Christ Himself! When Moses lift's up the rod, it is declaring to the enemy that no longer are my people under your authority but they are under God's authority! It is Christ and not the enemy that reigns over your life! It is Christ and not the enemy that Lords over your life! You have been bought with a price, Jesus Christ the propitiation for your sins! Lift up the ROD and show the devil who's boss! Lift up the Rod to show the devil who's in charge! Lift up the Rod and stop the devil in his tracks!

He lifts up the Rod, then he stretches out thine hand! And when he stretched out his hand the Lord caused the sea to go back by a strong east wind and made the sea, dry land! Father I stretch my hand unto thee no other help I know; if thou withdraw thyself from me, whither will I go! Lift up your Rod and Stretch Out your hand unto God! God's got you and God's got it!

Sermonette 2

He walks with You!

>» ———————————— «

Luke 24:13-31

We have just celebrated the highest and most sacred moments of a Faith – Resurrection Sunday! Indeed, we celebrate together as one church under one faith that Jesus died a real death and was buried in a real grave but what defines are Faith is the fact that the grave could not hold him! He got as He said on the third day with all power in His hand! He has risen! Christ has risen! However, it is the evening of Jesus resurrection that now piques my interest!

IN the text we find two of Jesus' disciples (one named Cleophas and the other unnamed) on a 7& ½ miles walk from the place of Jesus' death, burial and resurrection to a location village of which we only know is named Emmaus! They have heard that the tomb of Jesus was found empty earlier that day. They are discussing the events of the past few days and how they had hoped that Jesus had been the one which would have redeemed Israel! They discussed that certain women disciples who had been at the tomb early that morning had given them hope that Jesus was alive haven't been told by an angel that Jesus was not dead, He is a live! Why seek you the living amongst the dead but they doubted this because they hadn't seen Him with their own eyes! As they walked on towards Emmaus they discussed further and they doubted even more and while they talked together seemingly as stranger drew near and walked with them. The bible says that their eyes were holden that they should not know him. They had no idea that the person with whom they were walking was Jesus himself! Jesus listening to their discussion and perceiving their disbelief becomes grieved and expounds unto them all the scriptures concerning him.

There are some items of significance in this text that I believe the Lord would like to reveal to disciples today!

The first declaration that I'd like to share with you today is that Jesus is walking with them and they don't even know it! I submit to you today that it may not look like it! It may not feel like it and you might not recognize it but just as Jesus walked with and unbeknownst with the two disciples on that road to Emmaus, Jesus is walking with you today! You might not see it! You might not recognize it! You might not feel it but whatever journey you are on today, Jesus is walking right with you!

You might have been given a poor prognosis from your doctor but I want you to know that Jesus is walking right with you!

You might have been released unto hospice but I want you to know that Jesus is walking right with you! My bible says yea though walk through the valley of death thou are with me; thou rod and thy staff they comfort me!

Your marriage may be going through a real tough time right now and you feel like you are going to lose your mind but the Lord sent me here today to let you know that He is in it with you and you will not lose your mind! He will see you through!

You might have messed up, cheated, fallen off your spiritual journey but the Lord is walking right with you for He promised that He would never leave you nor forsake you! You might have left Him but He will never leave you!

You might have messed up in school this semester and you are wondering how you are going to turn it around! I've got good news for you! The Lord is walking with you! The Lord can and the Lord will take care of you!

You might be looking for a job and keep getting looked over! I've got news for you! The Lord has set aside the right job, at the right moment in time for you! In the mean time He's got you and He not suffer you to go under! The Lord is walking with you!

Secondly, it is significant that two, that's right two of Jesus' disciples are on this journey! You must understand that the number two means covenant but note that Jesus inserts himself into the walk and by doing so He minds us that a three-fold chord is not easily broken! Jesus is asserting to those who choose to follow him that regardless of what it looks like! Regardless of what you cannot see! Regardless of what you cannot comprehend! He is forever in covenant with you! All you have to do is invite Jesus into your situation and He will be the burden bearer for you! He will be the way maker for you! He will be your stronghold tower! Where the righteous run thereto and are saved!

Thirdly, it is significant that there are two disciples in this text but only one is named! One is named Cleophas but the other is un-named! I submit to you that Cleophas is the one that everybody knows! Cleophas is the one that everybody accepts! Cleophas is the one that everybody flocks to! But the un-named one! The un-named disciple is the one that is overlooked! He is the one that is not out front! He is the one that is always behinds the scenes but is faithfully serving! The one who is faithfully about his fathers' business! Jesus sent me all the way to 277 Madison Avenue this morning to speak to the nameless one! To speak to the title less one! To speak to the one who feels dejected and rejected! Jesus sent me to tell you that He sees you! Jesus sent me to tell you that He knows thy works! You might feel like you're overlooked! You might feel like no one cares! You might feel like no one sees you! But the Lord sent me here to day to tell you He sees you! He feels you! He knows your works! He knows your sacrifice! The last shall be first and the first shall be last! Touch your neighbor and declare the last shall be first and the first shall be last!

I'm about to close! I have to get out of here but before I go there is one more point of significance that I have to share with you! And it's in verse 29 where it says "But they constrained him, saying "Abide with us"! I hear the Lord saying Behold I stand at the door and knock! Any man who answers the door I will come into him and I will sup with him and he shall sup with me! You have got to invite Him in! You can't stand by the wayside and wait! You can't say I'll get around to it one day! You've got to invite Him while He can be found! Behold I stand at the door and knock! Any man who answers the door I will come into him and I will sup with him and he shall sup with me!

Verse 31 says after the y invited Him in and He supped with them "their eyes were opened and they knew him."

JUST A LITTLE TALK WITH JESUS!

I heard the psalmist say:

I once was lost in sin but Jesus took me in and then a little light

from heaven filled my soul.

It bathed my heart in love and wrote my above

And just a little talk with Jesus made me whole

Have a little talk with Jesus

Tell Him all about your troubles

He will hear our faintest cry and he will answer by and by

You my have doubts and fears my eyes be filled with tears

But Jesus is a friend who watches day and night

I go to Him in prayer He knows my every care

And just a little talk with Jesus makes it right

Poem

I'm black before I'm American, anything else makes no sense

Once in blackness ethnicity takes no precedence

I was born without chains, reared to roam free

My strength is within the divine, the divine is within me

Some same first American but my melanin steps ahead

Converts the mind of the unknowing and nothing else is said

It is interesting to note that from black all colors come

So, all who deprioritize my blackness, they themselves have shun

I'm happy to be American, proud to be black

My ethnicity secure; my darkness on track

RECITATION!

Say this out loud daily!

After All I've been through, Nothing can stop me!

Encoded in my DNA is a history of Overcoming!

My past is filled with culture, innovation, wealth ingenuity and

Excellence!

I am the Head and not the Tail!

I am Above and not Beneath!

I am human, dignified and wise!

God made me Intentionally and with Purpose!

I am the Hope of our future and of generations!

I am family-oriented, Responsible and Resourceful!

I no longer have to hide behind a mask, I am taking my rightful

place!

I will Build where I'm intended to Build!

I will Fulfill my Purpose and achieve Greatness!

I am More than a Conqueror!!!!

References Cited

»» ——————— ««

1. Kerr, ME, Bowen, M. Family Evaluation, An Approach Based On Bowen Theory; 1988 W. W. Norton & Company, Inc. New York, NY

2. Kunjufu, J. Black Economics, Solutions for Economic and Community Empowerment, 2nd edition, 1991 African American Images , Chicago, IL.

3. Cole, EL, Maximized Manhood, A Guide To Family Survival, 2001 Whitaker House, New Kensington, PA

4. Friedman, EH. Generation To Generation, Family Process In Church and Synagogue, 1985 The Guilford Press, New York, New York

5. Boyd-Franklin, N. Black Families in Therapy, Understanding The African American Experience, 2nd edition, 2003 The Guilford Press, New York, NY

6. Kornfeld, M. Cultivating Wholeness, A Guide to Care and Counseling in Faith Communities, 2005 The Continuum International Publishing Group, Inc, New York, NY

7. Wogaman, JP Christian Ethics, A Historical Introduction Westminster John Knox press, 1993 Louisville, Kentucky

8. McGoldrick, M You Can Go Home Again, Reconnecting with Your Family, 1995 W. W. Norton & Company, Inc. New York, NY

9. Bowlby 1958

10. National Center for Children in Poverty

11. U.S. Census Bureau, National Center for Health Statistics, Americans for Divorce Reform (www.divorcemag.com/statistics/statsUS.html)

12. Judith Lorber, "*Readings for Diversity and Social Justice*," Routledge, 2000, pg. 205

13. Warren J. Blumenfeld, "*Readings for Diversity and Social Justice*," Routledge, 2000, pg. 271

14. Paula c. Rodriguez Rust, "*Bisexuality in the United States*" Columbia University Press, 2000, pp 11-12

15. Janis S. Bohan & Glenda M. Russell, "Conversations About Psychology and Sexual Orientation", NYU Press, 1999, pg. 131

16. J.L. King, "*On the Down Low*" Harlem Moon, 2004

17. Monica McGoldrick, "*You Can Go Home Again*" W.W. Norton & Co., 1995, pg. 36

18. U.S. Department of Justice

19. The Bible (King James Version)

20. Bishop Donald Hilliard, Jr, Somebody Say Yes

21. Martin Luther Kings Letter from the Birmingham Jail

Additional Works Conferred

»» ———————— ««

Edwin H. Friedman, "Generation to Generation", The Guilford Press, 1985

Margaret Kornfield, "Cultivating Wholeness", The Continuum International Publishing Group, Inc., 2005

Ronald W. Richardson, "Creating a Healthier Church"

US Census 2000

Man Keung Ho, "Family therapy with Ethnic Minorities" Sage Publications, 1987

L. William Countryman, "Dirt, Gree, & Sex" Fortress Press, 1988

Elmer P. Martin and Joanne Mitchell Martin, "The Black Extended Family" University of Chicago Press, 1978

Marcus J. Borg, "Meeting Jesus Again for the First Time", HarperSanFrancisco, 1995

Laura Benkov, "Reinventing the Family" Crown Publishing, Inc., 1994

Gary David Comstock, "Unrepentant, Self-Affirming, Practicing", Continuum, 1996

Saba, Karrer, Hardy, "Minorities and Family Therapy" The Haworth Press, 1990

Mark JK Williams, "Sexual Pathways", Praeger Publishers, 1999